Brahmānanda Valli

Brahmānanda Valli

(Taittirīya Upaniṣad)

यथार्थ दशर्न

A perspective based on

Mind as a Mirror

Inspired by the divine teachings of
Bhagavan Sri Sathya Sai Baba

An Offering at the Divine Lotus Feet
by

Prof. O. S. K. S. Sastri

MLBD PUBLICATIONS

Motilal Banarsidass Publications

MOTILAL BANARSIDASS
PUBLICATIONS
4741/23, Ansari Road, Daryaganj, New Delhi - 110002 (India)
Email: mlbd@mlbd.com | sales@mlbd.com
exports@mlbd.com | publications@mlbd.com
Website: www.mlbd.com

Brahmānanda Valli
by
Prof. O. S. K. S. Sastri

First Edition Published in 2026

Published in India by Motilal Banarsidass Publications

ISBN : 978-93-7513-023-9 (PB)

Printed and bound in India

ॐ भूर्भुवः स्वः तत्सवितुर्वरेण्यं
भर्गो देवस्य धीमहि । धियो यो नः प्रचोदयात् ॥
ॐ शान्तिः शान्तिः शान्तिः ॥

ōṃ bhūr bhuvaḥ svaḥ, tat savitur varēṇyaṃ
bhargō dēvasya dhīmahi, dhiyō yō naḥ
prachōdayāt
ōṃ śhāntiḥ śhāntiḥ śhāntiḥ

(*Dhīmahi*) We meditate upon (*bhargō*) the spiritual effulgence (*varēnyam dēvasya*) of that adorable supreme divine reality, (*savitur*) the source of (*bhūḥ*) the physical (materialisation; body aspect), (*bhuvaḥ*) the astral (vibration; life force aspect), and (*svaḥ*) the heavenly spheres (radiation, *prajñā* or soul aspect) of existence. (*tat*) May that, (*yaḥ*) which is the supreme divine being, (*prachōdayāt*) enlighten (*naḥ*) our (*dhīyaḥ*) intellect, so that we may realize the supreme light.

An offering
at the Lotus Feet of
Bhagavan Sri Sathya Sai Baba

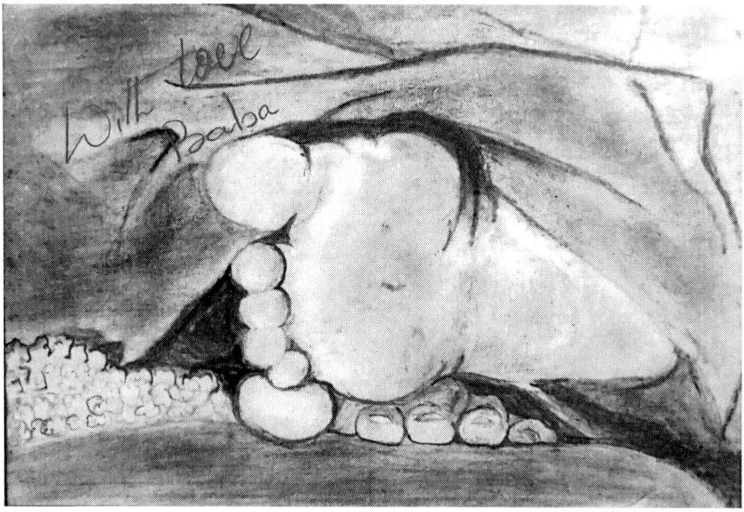

Contents

Foreword

Knowing *Brahman* or the Source of creation, experiencing it, and merging in it, is *Brahmānanda Vallī*'s way. This book gives insights into the path. To make things simple, the subtitle 'The Mind as a Mirror' is perfect. What if the mirror is not showing the right image? Will our perception of reality be distorted? If that happens, can graduating students be called educated?

Education was designed to give positions of responsibility in society to those who clear the examination. What is the examination? They should be able to distinguish the real from the unreal. If the unreal is mistaken as real, there will be conflict within the individual. The decisions, then taken, will lead to problems like social strife, threat of war, crime, and economic crisis.

What is the way to achieve *Brahmānanda*? How can education prepare students for it? For this, the mirror has to be set right. Three problems can arise with the mirror. First, the mirror is covered with dust. This is called *Mala*. The second problem can arise if the mirror is moving. Can the image be stable, then? This is the problem of *Vikṣepa*. The third problem is bigger. What if the mirror is covered with a dark cloth, and it sees the world as darkness? This problem is one relating to the six inner enemies. Apart from desire, greed, anger, attachment, envy, the enemy pride is the most difficult to overcome. This problem is called *Āvaraṇa*. Ancient wisdom recom-

mends regulating food, contemplation/meditation, and the practice of selfless love for conquering all of these, respectively. These practices are its real curriculum.
Prof. O. S. K. S. Sastri has brought about the inner research methodology to experience *Brahmānanda*, the ultimate. Only self-transformation leads to the experience of *Brahman* - which leads to, at one glance in any direction, '*knowing that one thing, knowing which, everything else can be known*'.

Satya Saurabh Khosla
18th September, 2025

Introduction

Brahmānanda Valli is one of the major *Upaniṣads* that deals with the knowledge of *Brahman*. It is said

"Ēkam Sat viprāḥ bahudā vadanti".

There is only One Truth, and Scholars describe it in a myriad ways.

This book is a comprehension of *Brahmānanda Valli*, the second chapter of the *Taittirīya Upaniṣad*. In the book '*Mantra Puṣpam*', a publication by Sri Ramakrishna Mission [1], this *Upaniṣad* is broadly divided into three parts.

The first part expands on the first *anuvāka* (paragraph) of the *Upaniṣad* and is titled "*Upaniṣad Sāra Saṅgraha*", "The Summary of the *Upaniṣad* in a precise form" or "The Essence of the *Upaniṣad* in Summary". In contemporary parlance, an Abstract.

The Second part, from 2nd to 7th *anuvākas*, is titled "*Pañcha Kośa Vivarṇam*", the description of the five sheaths which are the subtler layers of human existence.

The third and final part is the 8th *anuvāka*, which is titled "*Ānanda Mīmāṃsā*", "An Inquiry into the Nature of Bliss", followed by the Conclusion.

Hence, this book has also been divided into three chapters.

Chapter 1: *Puruṣa* ⇌ *puruṣa*

Chapter 2: How to Know One Self

Chapter 3: Levels of Bliss

Preface

The *Vēdas* are the main source of knowledge in *Bhāratiya Jñāna Parampara*. The *Upaniṣads* are part of *Vēdanta*, the culmination of the *Vēdas*. The central theme of all the *Upaniṣads* is knowledge of *Brahman*, the Ultimate Reality. There are 108 *Upaniṣads*, of which only 10 are considered major, as *Jagadguru Ādi Śaṅkarācārya* has written *bhāṣyas* for them. One of them is the *Taittirīya Upaniṣad*, the second portion of which is *Brahmānanda Valli*. It is mainly concerned with the exposition of the five sheaths or layers that encompass the Self. This book is an attempt to look at the entire content from the seeker's point of view.

This book is an epiphany that stuck while contemplating the nine *dravyās* of *Vaiśeṣika* philosophy [2]. In search of an answer to a question that arose in my mind as to how *Ṛṣi Kāṇāda* arrived at these nine *dravyās* of "*Ākāśa, Vāyu, Agni, Āpah, Pṛthvī, Dik, Kāla, Manas, and Ātmā*" as sufficient to explain the physical universe, the realisation dawned that the basis for the exposition is the *Vēdas*. In a flash, the recognition came that *Brahmānanda valli*'s first *anuvāka* consists of all of these, which has led to this exploration. I must confess that my knowledge of the *Vēdas* is limited to learning how to chant various *Suktams* given in the *Mantra Puṣpam* book by Sri Ramakrishna Mission. In my research, I have utilised the internet to obtain the meaning of Sanskrit words in the verses and added my understanding and consequent explanation.

In the process, I have considered the keywords *śiraḥ, dakṣiṇaḥ, uttaraḥ, ātmā,* and *puccham̱* to be adjectives instead of nouns. This resulted in understanding the *puruṣa*, human being, as the highest (*śiraḥ*) physical form of Creation. The twin capabilities of *karma* (*dakṣata*) and *jñāna* (*uttaraḥ*) endow the human being with the insight that one is the self (*ātman*). Hence, in culmination (*puccham̱*), the human being is consecrated (*pratiṣṭhā*) to be *Brahman* itself. This completed the Cycle of Creation, which gave me an internal validation.

A discussion with my colleague from the Sanskrit department in Central University of Himachal Pradesh, Dharamsala, evidenced that the existing interpretations considered these five terms to be nouns for describing the physical form of the human being. In the quest to cross-check, if the adjective interpretation remains valid for the rest of the *kośas*, newer insights inspired through my experiences with Bhagavan Sri Sathya Sai Baba, whom we reverentially address as *Swami*, opened a new dimension in my comprehension. Only after completing this endeavour have I read the original interpretations from various books mentioned in the references at the end of the book. It is important to remember that one's understanding is based on one's previous knowledge.

This book is mainly inspired by the loving guidance, experiences, and discourses of *Swami*. I have been blessed to be with my Divine Master from 1988 to 2011 in His *Brindavan ashram* at Whitefield, Bengaluru.

One should be unambiguous that the *Vēdas* do not need any validation from current Science. Being a student and teacher of Physics for over 30 years, I have presented my understanding and explanations from that perspective. For instance, the exposition of "God is Omnipresent" from the Fourier Transform perspective was inspired by my Professor while studying for my M.Sc. in 1991. Later, I developed the ideas presented in this book during my teaching tenure, as *Swami* said that we should integrate spirituality into our regular teaching of physics. A few of these have been incorporated, hopefully to pique the interest of current youth in spirituality.

In this book, the transition into each of the layers is looked upon as a transformation of the individual, by gaining an understanding of the *antaḥkaraṇa*, or the inner instrument. The various aspects of the mind are *manas, buddhi, chitta,* and *ahaṃkāra.* As one attains mastery over each of these aspects, one transitions across the inner layers of *Annamaya, Prāṇamaya, Manōmaya, Vijñānamaya*, and *Ānandamaya kośas.*

The process of knowing oneself involves knowing the One Self that expresses itself as all that exists in the Universe. Here, the *Taittirīya Upaniṣad* provides an inner methodology to experience the Self. Just as one needs a physical mirror to see one's face, so too does one have to utilise the mind as a mirror to see oneself, as the One Self. A physical mirror would have to be stable, illuminated, and clean to see one's face. Similarly, to see ourselves, the various facets of the mind, such as *manas, buddhi, chitta,* and *ahaṃkāra*, have to attain stability, illumination, purity, respectively, and ultimately, Unity. *Prāṇamaya kośa* culminates in *pṛthvī tattwam*, which is reflected as stability of the mind. That is, the *manas*, which is constantly filled with thoughts, akin to waves in a pond, needs to be stilled by controlling one's *prāṇa*. At this stage, one perceives the self to be luminous (*ākāśa ātmā*). The *Manōmaya kośa* culminates in *atharva (agni)* and *aṅgīrasa (āpaḥ) tattwas*, which are reflected as the purifying fire and insight obtained as the essence of various branches of knowledge. The knowledge of the *Vēdas* illumines the *buddhi* aspect of the mind with the insight that one is the *ātman* and not the body. The sincere practice of the *Vēdic* injunctions, in the form of *tapas*, purifies the *chitta* aspect of the mind. In this stage, the mind is stable, pure, and illuminated, and one can clearly indicate (*ādeśa*) the self within (*ādeśa ātmā*). Next, the *ahaṃkāra* aspect of the mind is overcome by living in constant integrated awareness through loving service to all beings, conscious of the underlying fundamental unity. This leads to the unity of the Self with the Divine (*yōga ātmā*). Finally, the individual self is dissolved in the One Self and is experienced as Bliss (*Ānanda ātmā*).

The interpretation of the five layers is comprehended in the *Ānanda Mīmāṃsā* as the enunciation of different levels of *Ānanda*. For example, at the very beginning of this *anuvāka*, it is declared that the Wind blows, the Sun rises, the Fire burns, Indra governs, and the Death hastens due to 'fear of' or 'reverent obedience' to *Brahman*. The Wind can be seen to be the breath, or *prāṇa* that stabilises the *manas*, the Sun, knowledge, which illumines the *buddhi*, the Fire that purifies the *chitta*, and *Indra*, the mind which attains union with the Divine. Finally, the dissolution of the individual self is indicated by stating that death hastens.

It has been an enlightening journey for me personally, and I hope readers enjoy this inner methodology of "How to know oneself as the One Self" and begin their own process of transformation.

Prof. O. S. K. S. Sastri

Acknowledgement

Offer myself at the Divine Lotus Feet of Bhagavan Sri Sathya Sai Baba. "He is the *Kartru* (Doer) and He is the *Bhoktru* (Enjoyer)". He is the divine poet who inspires all His works through us. While the beautiful symphony of ideas flows through us by His grace, the imperfections reflect the limitations of the instrument.

I am deeply grateful to my parents, Smt. O. Akhilandeswari and Sri. O. Seetha Ramayya and also my grandparents, Smt. O. Lakshmi Narasamamba and Sri. O. S. K. Subramanya Sastry (I am named after my grandfather). I am deeply grateful to my mother-in-law Smt. Sushila Padam for her love and affection. This work, like every other aspect of my life, is shaped by beautiful conversations with my better half, Dr. Anita Padam, who is a Professor of Physiology and Head at IGMC, Shimla. I also wish to express my love and affection to my brother Group Captain O. S. Narasimham VM, and my sister Smt. K. S. Annapurna for being in my life. I am grateful to all my teachers and relatives.

I thank Prof Avinash Chandra Pandey, Director of IUAC, New Delhi, for motivating me to work in Indian knowledge systems.

I thank my colleague, Prof. Brihaspati Mishra, Professor of Sanskrit, with whom the initial ideas for this book were developed. He helped my understanding of Sanskrit.

I am thankful to all my friends and students who have made my journey enjoyable. Their sincere efforts in listening to my reflections have brought much clarity into the formulation of ideas presented in this book. It has been a privilege to have wonderful, illuminating discussions with my friend Sri Satya Saurabh Khosla, who has been a constant source of motivation. My thanks to my student, M. R. Ganesh Kumar, for helping me with the Sanskrit Verse analysis software tool. I express my sincere thanks to Sri Y. Arvind for helping with editing. I would like to specially thank my research scholar, Mr. Ishwar Kant, who designed the front cover, the inside pages, and compiled the entire content of the book using the LaTeX scientific editor.

I am grateful to *SaiVeda* team from *www.saiveda.net* for providing the script of *Brahmānanda Valli* in both *Devanagari* and Roman Coloured Coding Script (RCCS) for melody and rhythm.

I am also grateful to Sri Pranav Jain, Motilal Banarasidas Publishing House, for partnering in this effort.

Prof. O. S. K. S. Sastri

1

Puruṣa ⇌ puruṣa

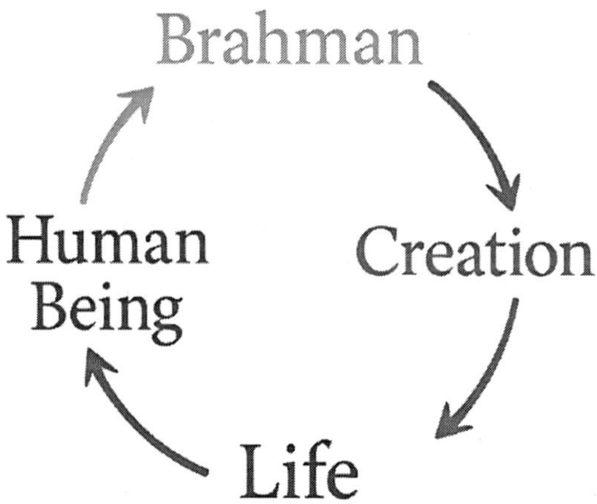

Śhāntipāthaḥa

ॐ स॒ह नांववतु । स॒ह नौंभुनक्तु। स॒ह वी॒र्यं॑ करवावहै।
ते॒ज॒स्विना॒वधींतमस्तु॒मा वि॑द्विषा॒वहैं॥
ॐ शान्ति॒ः शान्ति॒ः शान्तिः॑॥

om। saha nāvavatu। saha nau bhunak'tu।
saha vīr'yaṁ' karavāvahai।
tejas'vi nāvadhītamas'tu mā vidviṣhāvahaii।
om। śhān'tiśḥ' śhā-n'tiśḥ' śhā-n'tiḥi।।

Together let us move (Interact with each other)
Together let us relish (Enjoy the process of learning)
Together let us perform/pursue our studies with vigour or deep concentration (Sincerely Research)
May what has been Studied by us be filled with the Brilliance (of Understanding, leading to Knowledge)
May it Not give rise to Hostility (due to misunderstanding)

Upaniśhatsārasangrahaḥa

ब्रह्मविदाँप्नोति परमँ्। तदेषाऽभ्युंक्ता। सत्यं ज्ञानमंनन्तं ब्रह्मं।
Brahmavidāāp'nōti param'm [1.1]
tadēṣhā (a)bh'yuk'tā [1.2]
sat'yaṁ' jñānamanan'taṁ' brah'ma [1.3]
यो वेद निहिंतंगुहांयां परमे व्योंमन्।
सोँऽश्नुते सर्वान् कामाँन् सह। ब्रह्मंणा विपश्चितेतिं।
yō vēda nihitaṁ' guhāyāṁ' paramēv' vyōman'ne [1.4]
sōō'(a)śh'nutē sar'vān' kāmāān' saha,
brah'maṇā vipaśh'chitēti [1.5]
तस्माद्वा, एतस्मांदात्मनंआकाशः संभूंतः।
tas'mādvā, ētas'mādāt'mana, ākāśhas'saṁ'bhūtaḥa [1.6]
आकाशाद्वायुः। वायोरग्निः। अग्नेरापः। अद्भ्यः पृथिवी।
ākāśhād'vāyuḥu [1.7] vāyorag'niḥi [1.8]
ag'nērāpaḥa [1.9] ad'bhya[fp]' pṛthivī [1.10]
पृथिव्या, ओषंधयः। ओषंधीभ्योऽन्नमँ्। अन्नात्पुरुंषः।
स वा, एष पुरुषोऽन्न्नंरसमयः।
pṛthiv'yā , ōṣhadhayaḥa [1.11]
ōṣhadhīhbh'yō'(a)n'nam'm [1.12] an'nātpuruṣhaḥa [1.13]
sa vā, ēṣa puruṣhō'(a)n'narasamayaḥa [1.14]
तस्येदंमेव शिरः। अयं दक्षिंणः पक्षः। अयमुत्तंरः पक्षः। अयमात्माँ।
tas'yēdamēva śhiraḥ [1.15]
ayaṁ' dak'ṣhiṇaḥ[fp]' pak'ṣhaḥa [1.16]
ayamut'tara[fp]' pak'ṣhaḥa [1.17] ayamāt'māā [1.18]
इदं पुच्छँ प्रतिष्ठा। तदप्येष श्लोंको भवति।
idaṁ' puch'chhaṁ' pratiṣh'ṭhā [1.19]
tadap'yēṣhaś' śhlōkō bhavati [1.20]

The Central Theme

ब्रह्मविदाप्नोति परम्। ***Brahmavidāpnōti Param*** [1.1]

ब्रह्मविद् *Brahmavid* - The Knower of *Brahman* आप्नोति *āpnōti* - attains परम् *Param* - the Supreme

1.1 *The Knower of Brahman attains the Supreme.*

This statement sets the tone for the entire *Upaniṣad.* One can clearly decipher that the purpose of the content to follow is to charter a path that leads to *Param*, the Supreme.

Three questions arise:

Who is *Brahman*?

This is an ontological question.

How is *Brahman* known?

This is an epistemological question.

What is the Supreme that is attained?

This is an axiological question.

So, this is the goal of the seeker. To become *Brahmavid.* For, it is, what takes us to the true purpose of one's life, which is, to go back to the source from where we have come.

In *Chandōgya Upaniṣad* (3.2.9) [3], it is said that, '**ब्रह्मविद् ब्रह्मैव भवति** *Brahmavid brahmaiva bhavati*', the knower of *Brahman* becomes *Brahman* itself. Hence, one attains the state of *Brahman*, which is *mōkṣa* or immortality. *Mōkṣa* is *mōha kshaya*, the destruction of all attachment, which is a result of perceiving duality.

तदेषाभ्युक्ता। ***tadēṣābhyuktā*** [1.2]

तत् *tat* - That (above idea) अभ्युक्ता *abhyuktā* - has been declared एषा *ēṣā* - in this way;
1.2 *The following is said about the above.*

Who is *Brahman*?

सत्यं ज्ञानमनन्तं ब्रह्म।
Satyaṁ Jñānam Anantaṁ Brahma [1.3]

This implies "*Satyaṁ Brahma; Jñānam Brahma; Anantaṁ Brahma*". This aphorism has been elucidated in detail in the books by Swami Dayananda Saraswathi [4] and Sri Mahadeva Sastry [5]. Here, a very brief discussion based on the talk by by Swami Sarvapriyananda [6] has been presented.

अनन्तम् ब्रह्म *Anantaṁ Brahma*

अनंत *ananta* is न + अंत *Anantaṁ* Na - no + *Antaṁ* - limitation or end.
That which has no limitations or end.
One observes Three Limitations:

- **देश परिच्छेद** ***dēśa paricchēda***: Limitation of Space
- **काल परिच्छेद** ***kāla paricchēda***: Limitation of Time
- **वस्तु परिच्छेद** ***vastu paricchēda***: Limitation of Object

Brahman must be free of these limitations.

No limitation in Space implies **God is Omnipresent**

Every object occupies a certain space in the Universe, and there exists a vast amount of space that is separate from the object. Hence, every object is limited in space, as it occupies only a certain amount of space. *Brahman* is *anantaṁ* in space, which implies that no space in the universe is devoid of *Brahman*. Thus, *Brahman* is Omnipresent or *Sarva Vyāpi*, and occupies all of the space, both visible and invisible.

No limitation in Time implies **God is Eternal (Omniscient)**

Every object comes into existence at a certain point in time in the universe, stays or sustains itself for some time, and then gets annihilated or ceases to exist. Hence, every object in space has a limited time for which it exists. *Brahman* is anantaṁ in time, implying that it is eternal, *Nityam*, present at all times, past, present, and future. *Brahman* is hence Omniscient.

No limitation in Object implies **God is Non-dual (Omnipotent)**

Every physical object is unique and has distinct characteristics unlike any other. A pen can not be a laptop and vice versa. But *Brahman* cannot be an object that distinctly exists from any other object. It will become limited, and there may exist an object that it is not, creating a dichotomy that limits *Brahman* in space as well. *Brahman* is all objects without exception and is therefore non-dual, *Advaitam*, one without a second. Thus, everything or every object that exists is a visible manifestation of the invisible *Brahman* and hence is an indicator of Omnipotence.

This unlimited aspect of *Brahman* is experienced as *Ānanda* or Infinite Bliss.

सत्यं ब्रह्म *Satyaṁ Brahma*
Is *Brahman* Real?

Brahman is all-pervasive or Omnipresent, which means it must be everywhere. Means it must be **Here**. *Brahman* is eternal or Omniscient, meaning it must be at all times. Means it must be present **Now**.

Brahman is non-dual or *advaitam*, which means it must be everything or every entity. It means this laptop or this pen must be *Brahman*.

What is Real? Anything which exists is Real.

Satyam's root word is *Sat* meaning सत् - Existence

Existence satisfies all three characteristics of transcending the limitations of space, time, and object. Hence, *Brahman* as Existence is, in all space, at all times, and appears as all entities.

ज्ञानं ब्रह्म *Jñānam Brahma*

Conscious Experience is Knowledge. *Jñānam* requires both *Vṛtti* (Impressions on the mind) and चित् (Consciousness).

Does *Jñānam* satisfy the three requirements of *Anantaṁ*?

Consider body consciousness, laptop consciousness, and thought consciousness. Each is associated with a unique experience that is fleeting and not eternal. The common denominator for the experience is consciousness. Hence, it is consciousness that satisfies all three requirements. It transcends space, time, and object.

It is present wherever experience arises. It is always available in every moment. It is aware of all objects without being limited by them. Thus, **Chit or Consciousness** is ***Brahman***.

***Brahman* is described as:**

सत् चित् आनन्द स्वरूपः (*Sat-Chit-Ānanda Swarūpa*)

How to 'Know the *Brahman*'?

यो वेद निहितं गुहायां परमे व्योमन्।

yō vēda nihitaṁ guhāyāṁ paramē vyōman [1.4]

यो *yō* - That (*Brahman*) वेद *vēda* - is known निहितं *nihitaṁ* - as inherent गुहायां *guhāyāṁ* - within the cave (of *Buddhi*) as परमे व्योमन् *paramē vyōman* - Supreme *vyōman* (प्रज्ञा *Prajñā*). It is to be comprehended as Constant Integrated Awareness [7]. It is also understood as *Parama Prēma*, Supreme Love.

निहितं *nihitaṃ* - It's ever-present though never seen.

गुहायां *guhāyāṃ* - It's secretive as it is not apparent.

1.4 *That, Brahman, is known in the inherent cave of Buddhi as Prajñā, Constant Integrated Awareness.*

Where is the *Brahman* Known?

One knows or experiences anything only within oneself. We see an object through our eyes and come to know it through the impression created on the brain as a perception, and comprehend it with the *buddhi*, an aspect of the mind (due to *Prajñā* or Consciousness). Similarly, the *Brahman* has to be experienced inherently in the cave of the *Buddhi*.

From a physiology perspective, *nihitham guhāyāṁ* is a cave-like structure located in the middle of the brain, which is the third ventricle [8] **filled with cerebrospinal fluid. It is in front of the pineal gland.**

Philosophically, this is understood as the spiritual center, where the *Brahman* is known or experienced as *paramē vyōman*.

What is *paramē vyōman*?

To understand *vyōman*, one needs to know what is *Ākāśa*. In *Sāṅkhya Darśana* [9], *vyōman* is given a numerical value of 0 while *Ākāśa* is given 1. ***vyōman* is the '*tattwa*' (fundamental principle) of *Ākāśa*.** *vyōman* is *adhāra* (fundamental basis) for *Ākāśa*, which is *ādhēya*

(existing entity).
For example, the basis for water, which is visible, is Hydrogen and Oxygen, which are unseen.
Similarly, *vyōman* cannot be perceived, but it can be experienced as *Ākāśa.*

What is *Ākāśa*?

आकाशः (*ākāśa*): the root word is '*kas*' to shine brightly (light or effulgence), and the prefix '*a*' conveys the sense of *samānatā maryādā*, which means limit all-around [10]. **Hence, *ākāśa* is the entire field within the limit of light, called space.**

A question may arise: If *ākāśa* is interpreted as the field of light, then why is it seen as dark at night?
The human eye is not sensitive to seeing actual light rays. It can only see the source of light or that reflected from an object.
Example: On a full moon night, the moon appears to shine brightly. But, we do not see any rays of sunlight falling upon the moon.

What is the fundamental principle that governs the concept of *Ākāśa*?

Today, light is known to be electromagnetic energy. Since *Ākāśa* is the entire space filled with light, its fundamental basis, *vyōman*, can be considered as the field of electromagnetic energy, typically referred to as the zero-point energy or quantum vacuum.

How is the *paramē vyōman* experienced?
In *Puruṣa Suktham* [1], chapter 31 of *Yajurvēda*, it is declared as follows:

वेदाहमेतं पुरुषं महान्तम्, आदित्यवर्णं तमसः परस्तात्।
vedāhametaṁ puruṣaṁ mahāntam
ādityavarṇaṁ tamasaḥ parastāt

अहम् *aham - I have* वेद *vēda - known (not intellectually, but through direct experience),* एतम् *etam - this,* पुरुषम् *puruṣam - the Being* माहान्तम् *māhāntam - (who is) Supreme or Infinite or Limitless, that is, Brahman,* आदित्यवर्णम् *ādityavarṇam - (as) brilliant effulgence of the Sun, that is, self-luminous pure consciousness,* परस्तात् *parastāt - beyond or by transcending* तमसः *tamasaḥ - the darkness of ignorance.*

I have known the Brahman as Self-luminous, pure consciousness beyond the darkness of ignorance.

So, *paramē vyōman* is experienced as *Ākāśa* only.

God is Omnipresent, Omniscient, and Omnipotent

A Physics Perspective:

Particle: A particle has a finite spatial extent and exchanges energy instantaneously in a collision.

Wave: A wave, on the other hand, has in principle an infinite spatial extent and exchanges energy over a wavelength during interaction with matter.

Typically, when two or more particles come together, they form a group even while retaining their identity, but when two or more waves superimpose together, they tend to produce regions of constructive and destructive interference.

Hence, it is extremely difficult to comprehend a particle displaying wave nature and vice versa.

Yet, it is observed clearly in daily interactions. While our physical body exhibits a particle nature, the language we speak, due to thoughts that are formulated in our mind, is articulated in the form of waves of sound that traverse far beyond our physical boundaries.

Wave-Particle Duality

The interaction of light with matter shows that it behaves as both a particle and a wave, which is called wave-particle duality .

Similarly, our observations in Physics have revealed that all matter at the fundamental level consists of elementary particles, such as electrons, which also behave as Waves.

Finally, to accommodate both the natures of light, the concept of a wavepacket has been proposed. The wave associated with a particle is constructed as a superposition of an infinitely large number of waves with infinitesimally close frequencies, so that the resultant is a wavepacket of finite spatial extent as required by the concept of particles.

The amplitude function that multiplies these waves is unique to each particle and gives rise to the variety or diverse particles in nature. This superposition is mathematically expressed as a Fourier transform .

The amplitude function is a function in the frequency (spatial or temporal) domain, and its Fourier transform, which is the superposition or addition of an infinitely large number of waves that have infinitesimally close frequencies, is an integral that results in the wavepacket in the space-time domain. The inverse integral can also be constructed and is called the inverse Fourier transform. One of the most important and interesting superpositions is obtained when the amplitude function F(k) is a Gaussian function, which is a bell-shaped curve, as shown on the right-hand side (RHS) of Figure 1. It's important because most of the phenomena in nature are seen to be bell-shaped, and it's interesting because its Fourier trans-

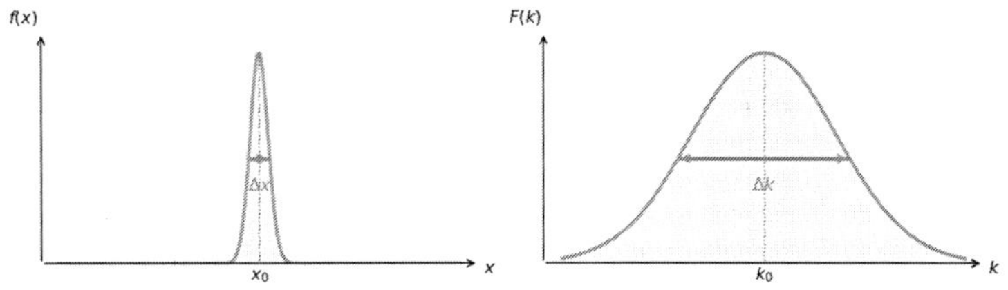

Figure 1.1: **RHS**: The Gaussian function in k-space with width Δk acting as amplitude function and **LHS**: Fourier transform of Gaussian function in k-space, with Δk, results in a Gaussian function in x-space, with width Δx, such that $\Delta x \times \Delta k = 1$.

form is another Gaussian function (See the left-hand side (LHS) of Figure 1). The most interesting aspect is that the width of the Gaussian function (represented as Δx) in the space domain is inversely related to the width of the Gaussian function (represented as Δk) in the spatial frequency domain. That is, $\Delta x \Delta k = 1$, which is the uncertainty relation with minimum value, when multiplied by $\hbar$ on both sides. The smaller the width in the space-time domain, the larger the width in their respective Fourier domains. When the width of the Gaussian function with unit area tends to zero, with the total area under the curve remaining as unity, we call the resulting function a Delta function, see LHS of Figure 2. One must keep in mind that this is only conceptual and such a function does not exist in reality. The Fourier transform of such a Delta function would become a Constant function in the Fourier domain, as shown on RHS of Figure 2.

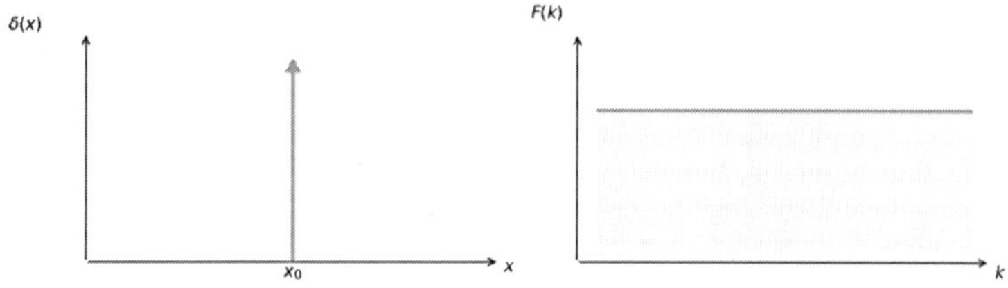

Figure 1.2: **LHS**: When the width of the Gaussian function in x-space tends to zero, one obtains a delta function, and **RHS**: the width of the Gaussian function in k-space will tend to infinity, resulting in a Constant function.

Interpretation

Ahaṃkāra **- Body Consciousness:** *Ahaṃ Akāram* means that I am this *Ākāram* (form), which constitutes the Body-Mind-Intellect (BMI) complex. This misidentification is called the Ego. The BMI complex is formulated here, mathematically, as a Gaussian wavepacket, in the space-time domain, whose width is interpreted to be the Ego.

Prajñā **-** ***Ātmic*** **Consciousness:** *Prajñā* is the Constant Integrated Awareness (CIA) which makes one realise that one's true nature is *Ātma* and the same *Ātma* is present in all other living beings.

One's *Prajñā* is related to BMI through the Fourier Transform. One's *Prajñā* is also a Gaussian wavepacket in the respective spatio-temporal frequency domains, whose width can be interpreted as the Spiritual Quotient

(SQ), the capability to see the Oneness. So, SQ and Ego are inversely related.

The human being who is an embodiment of consciousness, considered as the *ātman*, has the aspects of Body, Mind, and Intellect (BMI). Ego is the identification or superposition of consciousness (spirit) with this BMI complex. Currently, we tend to measure some of these implicitly embodied personality traits with what we call an Intelligence Quotient (IQ), reflecting one's sharpness of mind, and an Emotional Quotient (EQ), which assesses a person's capability to build rapport and work in teams, which requires the art of empathy and openness. The rationalistic thought is yet to understand the importance of Spiritual Quotient (SQ), which is to understand that the same Consciousness present in all is the source that makes us think, talk, listen, do, and be. Spirituality is a transformation process from animality to humanity to divinity. Unfortunately, the person lives in an elusive state wherein one thinks that one is the body. This wrong identification of a person being the body, while in reality one is the *ātman*, is what is termed as *ahaṃkāra* (*ahaṃ akāram*) or ego. When a person is steeped in body consciousness, they are driven by self-interest and selfishness. One is always influenced and misled by the feelings of mine and thine, leading to attachment with people, things, and concepts. This results in compartmentalization and divisiveness, which makes us relate to certain people and not all of mankind. On the other hand, those who 'believe' or 'are capable of perceiving' in the unity beyond the apparent diversity develop unconditional love for all humanity. One can easily appreciate the above when one reflects on ideas of 'wavelength' or 'frequency' matching, which are referred to in common conversation.

The Parallel between Gaussian Widths: *Ahaṃkāra* and Spiritual Quotient

The Gaussian function can be associated with the general conscious state of the person in the space-time domain, with its width specifying, say, the *ahaṃkāra* aspect of the embodied person and its Fourier transform, which is also a Gaussian function in the frequency domain, which shall represent one's personality with its width specifying the Spiritual Quotient (SQ).

When *ahaṃkāra*, the width in the space-time domain, is very small, then the person's SQ will be reflected as a larger width in the frequency domain. Hence, one can vibe with many more people of different frequencies; that is, one could have a greater circle of love in the frequency or Fourier domain. So, if there were to be a person who is steeped in *ātmic* consciousness and has negligible body consciousness, whom we refer to as realized souls, their Gaussian function in space-time would have negligible width, meaning, they are always in the Here and Now, and they are in tune with beings with different frequencies and thus love all mankind. Hence, if a realized soul can be considered to be a delta function in the space-time domain, the domain of the BMI complex, then such a person develops attributes of GOD, such as Omnipresence, Omnipotence, and Omniscience in the frequency or Fourier domain, the domain of the spirit. So, Omnipresent and Omniscient here implies being present in spirit everywhere and at all times, which is not in the space-time domain but in the spatio-temporal frequency domains. Similarly, Omnipotence means equally potent everywhere, which is true, as the Fourier transform of a delta function results in a Constant function, with equal magnitude, at all frequencies in the Fourier domain. Hence, one who is in *ātmic* consciousness equally loves all, irrespective of their differences.

Love is GOD, Live in Love

Our conscious state is limited by our ability to be or not to be in the present moment, completely. Generally, we tend to lose ourselves in memories of the past or apprehensions about the future, and are most often impeded by burdens or experiences from the past (referred to as *vāsanās*), that colour our vision of the present with a filter of opinions and perceptions arising from our past, and not as completely independent and fresh events. We are influenced by our previous circumstances and tend to observe the current situation with a filtered perspective. This limits our capacity and capability to be completely present in the moment, experience, and participate in the pure magic of Love, and hence, miss the present, which is indeed Omnipresent.

As we tend to reach a state of no thoughts (*amanaśka*), we would become more aware and Be, a conscious state where we see the unity of beings and are not lost in Becoming. So, being in the here and now (*Īśāvāsyamidam Sarvam*) makes us attuned to whatever there is in the moment and makes us accept the moment in Toto without reservations, and that is true Love and is the way to understand that Love is GOD and Live in Love.

Here and Now

Consider this sentence: **God is nowhere**
An atheist reads it as 'God is no where'
A theist reads it as 'God is now here'

Personal Experience

What *Sādhanā* to do?
Having read the book "**Purifying the Heart** [11]" I was inspired to undertake *Sādhanā* or Spiritual Practice
.

Bhagavan Sri Sathya Sai Baba (whom we lovingly call as '*Swami*'), came in my dream, and we were all seated in *Trayee Brindavan*, the residence of *Swami*, inside *Brindavan ashram* at Kadugodi, Bengaluru.
All of us are chanting *vēdam*.
Not many were able to join as the *mantra* is tough.

Swami got up and went inside.
I told Nandagopal Sir, my roommate in the hostel and our librarian, who is in charge of *vēdam* chanting in *Brindavan*, that let us change the *mantra* to something simple so that many more can join the chanting. So, we changed the chanting to *Sivōpāsana mantra* [1] as *Swami* entered.
Swami came back and sat in the *Joola* (swing) and enjoyed the chanting.
Then, *Swami* called me: Hey! Boy! Come here!
Krishna *kada* (in Telugu, my mother tongue), is your name not Krishna?
"Yes, *Swami*," I said.
Swami asked, **"What do you want"?**
I said, **"*Swami*! Devotion to your Lotus feet"**.
Swami signaled to me to take *pāda namaskāram* (touching the Lord's feet with devotion and love), and I have taken it happily.
While returning to my place, where I was sitting, I remembered about *Sādhana*. So, I turned back and said **"Swami! Sādhana cheyyali"**, that is, **"*Swami!* I want to do *Sādhana*"**
Swami Said, "*Emi cheyakkara ledu Bangāru! Ikkada Vundu; Chālu*"
"*Oh! Bangāru* (Dear one) ! No need to do anything, be here, that's enough. "
At that time in 2005, I had thought that 'be here' meant to be in *Brindavan* with *Swami*, in His Fold, and that's

all that is needed. He will take care of everything. Nothing else needs to be done. This indeed was true.

Later, after *Swami* had taken *Mahāsamādhi* in 2011, as per *Swami*'s guidance in three clear dreams, I had shifted to Himachal Pradesh, after staying close to 25 years with Him at *Brindavan.* Leaving *Brindavan* has been extremely tough, and I was somehow internally disturbed all the time and felt that I had lost a golden opportunity to serve there for life. I was always troubled with these two different dreams: One, in which *Swami* gave me a simple *sādhana* to be in *Brindavan*, and another, in which He guided me to go to Himachal.

Recently, I was giving lectures on Indian Knowledge Systems, in which a brief introduction to the *Upaniṣads* needed to be delivered. This allowed me to browse through the major *Upaniṣads*, and one of them is the *Ishavāsya Upaniṣad.* It starts with the following;

ईशा वास्यमिदं सर्वं यत्किञ्च जगत्यां जगत्।

(*Īśa*) *Īśvara* is, (*vāsyam*) residing or present (*sarvam*) everywhere and (*yat kiñcit*) whatsoever exists (that is in everything), (*Jagatyām Jagat*) in this world, (*idam*) is in the here and now. That is, *Īśvara* is Omnipresent, in the here and now.

During my morning prayer, when I was sitting silent, my dream in which I had asked *Swami* for *sādhanā* surfaced, and yet once I had realised that *Swami* said, "*ikkada vundu chālu*", which meant "**Be Here, that's enough**".

To be in the here and now is the true *sādhana.*
My heart felt very elated, and at the same time, my confusion got cleared. Whatever *Swami* says is Truth and is relevant at all times.

What is the Supreme that is attained?

सोऽश्नुते सर्वान् कामान् सह, ब्रह्मणा विपश्चितेति ॥
sō'śnutē sarvān kāmān saha,
brahmaṇā vipaśchitēti [1.5]

सः *saḥ* - One who knows the *Brahman* अश्नुते *aśnutē* - attains or enjoys सर्वान् *sarvān* - all कामान् *kāmān* - desires सह *saha* - together with ब्रह्मणाविपश्चित *brahmaṇāvipaśchita* - all knowing *Brahman* इति *iti* - thus.
1.5 *One who knows the Brahman enjoys all the desires, together with the all-knowing Brahman.*
The same verse also conveys the intent of *Brahmavid* and *Brahman* to create all that exists, so that they can enjoy everything together when read from right to left. This leads to a new interpretation revealing the reason behind the Creation.

Why this Creation?

सोऽश्नुते सर्वान् कामान् सह, ब्रह्मणा विपश्चितेति ॥
sō'śnutē sarvān kāmān saha,
brahmaṇā vipaśchitēti [1.5]

इति *iti* - Thus, ब्रह्मणाविपश्चित *brahmaṇāvipaśchita* - inspired by the all-knowing *Brahman*, सः *saḥ* - *Brahmavid* and *Brahman* कामान् *kāmān* - desires (to become) सर्वान् *sarvān* - all (everything that exists) to अश्नुते *aśnutē* - enjoy सह *saha* - together.

1.5 ***Thus, inspired by the all-knowing Brahman, Brahmavid, along with Brahman, desired to become all that exists, this entire universe, to enjoy together.***

Swami said, *"I separated Myself from Myself, so that I may love Myself."* This interpretation connects smoothly to the next few verses, which explain the process of Creation, the Evolution of Human Being, and the Purpose of Life.

Process of Creation

तस्माद्वा एतस्मादात्मन आकाशः संभूतः।

tasmādvā ētasmādātmana ākāśasaṃbhūtaḥ [1.6]

तस्मात् *tasmāt* - Hence, वा *vā* - indeed, truly एतस्मात् *ētasmāt* - for this specific reason of desiring to become many आत्मनः *ātmanaḥ* - from the Self आकाशः *ākāśaḥ* - the entire field of the limit of light, called space सम्भूतः *sambhūtaḥ* - emerged or originated.

1.6 ***Hence, from the Self originated ākāśa.***

According to *Sāṅkhya*, its attribute is शब्द (*śabda*), that denotes आविष्कार (*āviṣkāra*) and भाषण (*bhāṣaṇa*). The term '*avis*' means making visible something which is/was already in existence but invisible, and '*kara*' means been or being done. That is, *āviṣkāra* means making it visible or manifestation. So,*ākāśa* is the field of space that manifests the visible Universe.

Bhāṣaṇa means discourse. This speech is capable of riding on the electromagnetic (EM) waves travelling to the very limits of light soundlessly. That is, *ākāśa* is full of EM waves modulated by sound.

Just as our eyes are incapable of seeing the light-filled *ākāśa*, so also our ears can not hear these sound vibrations that modulate over the EM waves and fill all space. One may opine that these sound vibrations are the *Vēdas* that our *ṛṣis* have been able to perceive in their meditation. Hence, the *Vēdas* are declared as अपौरुषेय - *Apauruṣēya*, not of human origin.

आकाशाद्वायुः। वायोरग्निः। अग्नेरापः। अद्भ्यः पृथिवी।
ākāśādvāyuḥ [1.7], vāyoragniḥ [1.8], agnērāpaḥ [1.9], adbhyahpṛthivī [1.10]

1.7 *From Ākāśa came into existence Vāyu*

This is the second *mahābhūta*, which can be understood as force or equivalently motion. It also went on to represent the gaseous state in the atmosphere or the *prāṇa* within our body.

1.8 *From Vāyu came into existence Agni.*

This is the third *mahābhūta*. Here, it refers to the thermonuclear processes that are observed in stars such as the Sun. The other references to *agni* are the plasma state and the *Jatarāgni*, the fire within the stomach.

1.9 *From Agni came forth Āpah.*

This has been explained as constituting the processes of various nuclear reactions. *Āpah* also came to be known as water, but one must not limit its meaning to just water. It represents all liquid states of matter.

1.10 *Pṛthvī originated from Āpah.*

This culminates in the achievement of the final stable states of matter in the form of molecules. One should not limit its meaning to just connotating Earth, but it should include all planets and other non-stellar bodies. Later, it takes on the meaning of a solid state of matter as well. But, here as a *mahābhūta*, it is purely only a process of formation of bonds between atoms to bring about stable molecules.

One can obtain an elaborate discussion on these **mahābhūtas** in the book titled "***Vēdic Physics***" by Keshav Dev Verma [10].

The process of creation is variously described in the ōēdas to elaborate on the principle of *Brahman* through three names [7]:

विराट *Virāṭa*, the manifested form of God as the Universe.

हिरण्यगर्भ *Hiraṇyagarbha*, the Golden Womb from which all creation manifested, and

अव्याकृत *Avyākṛta*, the formless God beyond Creation.

These three forms relate to the gross, subtle, and causal, and the waking, dream, and deep-sleep states.

The नासदीयसूक्तम् *Nāsadīya Sūktam*, Hymn of Creation, is the 129th hymn of the 10th मंडल *maṇḍala* of the ऋग्वेद *ṛgvēda* (10:129) [12]. It is concerned with Cosmology and the Origin of the Universe and describes the form of God beyond Creation, अव्याकृत *Avyākṛta.*

Similarly, the हिरण्यगर्भ सूक्तम् *Hiraṇyagarbha Sūktam* is the 121st hymn of the 10th *mandala* of the ऋग्वेद *ṛgvēda* (10:121) [12]. It means the golden womb, which is considered the source of the creation of the Universe.

The पुरुष सूक्तम् *Puruṣa Sūktam* is there in all four vēdas and appears as Chapter 31 of the यजुर्वेद *yajurvēda* [13]. *Puruṣa* is defined as "पुरी सर्वेस्मिन् संसारे अभिव्याप्य सीदति वर्त्तते इति" (*purī sarvesmin saṃsāre abhivyāpya sīdati varttte iti*) that which exists pervading and engulfing the entire cosmic system and can be considered as the *Virāt Swarup* of *Brahman.*

In *Sāṅkhya darshana* (1/61) [9], *Prakṛti* is defined as:

"*Sattva-rajas-tamasām sāmyāvasthā prakṛtih*"

Sattva is existence, *rajas* connotes motion, and *tamas* is an inclination to transform or condense. *Sāmyāvasthā* is the state of being that remains the same or is conserved.

Hence, *Prakṛti* is that which in any of its three

states, of existence, motion, and transformation or condensation to some other form, remains the same.

But, it is also described as *Jada* (inertial), and hence cannot do anything on its own. Further, *Prakriti* is considered as the *Upādānakāraṇa* or the material cause of the Universe, and it's first great work is the *Mahat*, which means to arouse. *Prakriti*, being *Jada*, is incapable of any activity. Hence, the source of the stimulus is considered to be from *Puruṣa*, which is the instrumental or efficient cause, and the result is the appearance of *Hiranya Garbha*.

Now, one can observe that *ākāśa* is similar to *Prakṛti*. Both are *Jada*. The only difference is, while *ākāśa* has emerged from ātman (equivalent of *Puruṣa*), *Prakṛti* is already in a state of existence. *Vāyu*, which came from *ākāśa*, is the universal force that brought forth the rest of the universe in the field of *ākāśa*. In *Sāṅkhya*, it is *Puruṣa* who arouses *Prakṛti*, gives birth to *Mahat*, which consists of the entire blueprint of the Universe. Hence, one can interconnect the two concepts of *Mahat* and *Vāyu* and see that both of them represent the intelligence principle that sets into motion the creation of the Universe in all its expanse.

Evolution of Life on Earth

पृथिव्या ओषधयः। *pṛthivyā ōṣadhayaḥ* [1.11]

पृथिव्य *pṛthivya* - From Earth अयः *ayaḥ* - has come ओषधि *ōṣadhi* - (अ *a* -limited by + उष *uṣa* - heat due to Sun's radiation + धि *dhi* represents धातु *dhātu* to hold).

So, ओषधि *ōṣadhi* - is that which bears the heat due to Sunlight and is limited by it.

1.11 ***From Earth, emerged plant life.***

From Earth, the entire plant life has come into existence due to radiation from Sunlight captured as heat.

ओषधीभ्योऽन्नम्। *ōṣadhībhyō'nnam* [1.12]

ओषधिः *ōṣadhiḥ* - From plant life अयः *ayaḥ* - has come अन्नम् *annam* - food.

1.12 ***Food has come forth from the plant life.***

The implied meaning of Annam is Annamaya śarīra, that is, the physical forms that are a product of food and are sustained by it. This refers to various physical forms of birds, animals, insects, and all living beings that are sustained by food.

अन्नात्पुरुषः। *annātpuruṣaḥ* [1.13]

अन्नात् *annāt* - From food; पुरुषः *puruṣaḥ* - human being;

1.13 ***From food has come the human being.***

From among those living beings that are born through evolutionary stages of various combinations came forth the human being.

स वा एष पुरुषोऽन्न्नरसमयः।

sa vā ēṣa puruṣō'nnnarasamayaḥ [1.14]

स वा एष *sa vā ēṣa* - In that endeavour (of creation of life) अन्नमय *annamaya* - the physical form of पुरुष *puruṣa* - human being (has emerged) रसः *rasaḥ* - as the essence.

1.14 *In that endeavour, of creation of life, the puruṣa has emerged as the essence.*

Typically, this is translated as "*Verily, man, this human being, is made of the essential substance of food*". This is because the last part *annnarasamayaḥ* is broken as *anna* + *rasamayah.* Whereas, here it is taken as *annamaya* + *rasah.* Thus, this gives a new interpretation that, "**The human being is the essence of all physical forms in Creation**".

तस्येदमेव शिरः। ***tasyēdamēva śiraḥ*** [1.15]

तस्य *tasya* - Of that इदम् *idam* - this is एव *ēva* - indeed शिरः *śiraḥ* - the head.

1.15 *Of that puruṣa, this indeed is the Head.*

One can interpret the शिरः *śiraḥ* (head) as an adjective instead of a noun. Then, it would mean peak or highest.

The form of human being is indeed the highest (form of creation). Why?

The implied meaning of शिरः *śiraḥ* could be taken as the brain, which is what is inside the head. The size of the brain to the size of the body in the human being is today known in physiology to have an appropriate ratio of 1:50 [14, 15]. This makes the human being supreme among all beings.

Emergence of *Puruṣa*

From Earth, the entire plant life has come into existence due to the radiation from the Sunlight captured as heat.
The various physical forms of birds, animals, insects, and all living beings that are sustained by food have emerged from the plant life.
From among those living beings that are born through evolutionary stages of various combinations came forth the human being.
In nature's endeavour of creation of life, the physical form of puruṣa, the human being, has emerged as the essence and is indeed the highest.

Description of Human Being

तस्येदमेव शिरः।

tasyēdamēva śiraḥ [1.15]

तस्य *tasya* - Of that इदम् *idam* - this is एव *ēva* - indeed शिरः *śiraḥ* - the head.

1.15 *Of that puruṣa, this indeed is the head.*

One can interpret the शिरः *śiraḥ*(head) as an adjective instead of a noun. Then, it would mean peak or highest.

The form of human being is indeed the highest (form of creation).

अयं दक्षिणः पक्षः। अयमुत्तरः पक्षः।
ayaṃ dakṣiṇaḥ pakṣaḥ **[1.16]**
ayamuttaraḥ pakṣaḥ **[1.17]**

Here, we observe a shift, not grammatically, but phenomenologically, from **इदम्** *idam* - Object (known) in the third-person sense to **अयं** *ayaṃ* - Subject (knower) in the first-person sense.

दक्षिणः पक्षः *dakṣiṇaḥ pakṣaḥ* - as 'direction' is 'South', as a 'Limb' is 'Right side', as 'an attribute' is 'dexterity', 'skill', 'capability', and as a 'ritual' it is 'fee or honorarium'.
Hence, it may be interpreted as:

1.16 ***The right side***, in a spatial or anatomical sense, of the physical body of the human being.

Or alternatively as,

1.16 ***"The capable side" or "active/efficient aspect"*** (metaphorically). The side of action, ability, or Karma.

उत्तरः पक्षः *uttaraḥ pakṣaḥ* - as 'direction' is 'North', as a 'Limb' is 'Left side', as 'a sequence' is 'later or subsequent', as a qualitative 'attribute' is 'higher', 'superior', and from 'logical point of view', it is 'the answer' or 'response-position'.

Hence, it may be interpreted as:

1.17 ***"The left side"*** (if you're facing east)

Or alternatively as,

1.17 ***"The superior or higher side"*** the aspect of ascent, contemplation, transcendence. Hence, it can be viewed as the side of *jñāna* (knowledge), *mōkṣa* (liberation), or higher purpose.

अयमात्मा। *ayamātmā* [1.18]

अयं *ayaṃ* - This (here) is the अत्मा *atmā -ātman* (Self).

1.18 ***The person can know that one is the Self.***

इदं पुच्छं प्रतिष्ठा। *idaṃ pucchaṃ pratiṣṭhā* [1.19]

There is a shift from *ayaṃ* back to *idam*, here.

पुच्छं pucchaṃ - Tail **प्रतिष्ठा** pratiṣṭhā - Final resting point, the grounding or foundation, that which supports.

1.19 ***This tail is the support or foundation.***

<u>Physical Perspective of Annamaya Śarīra:</u>

तस्येदमेव शिरः। *tasyēdamēva śiraḥ* - This is the **Head**.

अयं दक्षिणः पक्षः। *ayaṃ dakṣiṇaḥ pakṣaḥ* - This is **right** side.

अयमुत्तरः पक्षः। *ayamuttaraḥ pakṣaḥ* - This is **left side**.

अयमात्मा। *ayamātmā* - This is the **center**.

इदं पुच्छं प्रतिष्ठा। *idaṃ pucchaṃ pratiṣṭhā* - This **tail**

is the support or foundation.

Typically, the interpretations consider these five terms, "*śiraḥ, dakṣiṇaḥ, uttaraḥ, ātmā* and *puccham*" to be nouns and give the meanings as "Head, Right, Left, Center, and Tail", respectively.

Here, two alternative interpretations are provided. At the intellectual level, one is inspired by the fact that the size of the brain-to-body ratio plays an important role in evolution, and hence it is interesting to consider the description to be that of the brain. Second, at the philosophical level, it is important to understand why the human being is uniquely privileged to obtain the Supreme.

Physiological Perspective Annamaya Śarīra:

तस्येदमेव शिरः। *tasyēdamēva śiraḥ* - The head implies the brain. So, the top part of the brain or the head can be construed as the **Cerebral Cortex**, which is responsible for all the neurological processes in the brain.

अयं दक्षिणः पक्षः। अयमुत्तरः पक्षः।
ayaṃ dakṣiṇaḥ pakṣaḥ; ayamuttaraḥ pakṣaḥ
These are the **right and left hemispheres** of the brain. While the right hemisphere is responsible for creativity, talent, emotions, and feelings, the left hemisphere is into reasoning, mathematical ability, and synthesis.

अयमात्मा। *ayamātmā* - This is the Center of the brain, **the third ventricle**.

इदं पुच्छं प्रतिष्ठा। ***idaṃ puccham pratiṣṭhā*** - The tail is the **medulla oblongata** followed by the Spinal Cord.

Philosophical Perspective Annamaya Śarīra:

तस्येदमेव शिरः। ***tasyēdamēva śiraḥ***
This, human form, is indeed the highest (form of creation).

अयं दक्षिणः पक्षः। ***ayaṃ dakṣiṇaḥ pakṣaḥ*** *- This is the "capable side", the side of action, or Karma.*

अयमुत्तरः पक्षः। ***ayamuttaraḥ pakṣaḥ*** *- This is the "higher side", the side of higher purpose, or Jñāna.*

These two aspects bestow human beings with *Jñāna* (Wisdom) and *Karma* (Action with intent) that set them apart from the rest of creation.
अयंआत्मा। ayaṃātmā *This is the Self. The inner witness, present in all experiences.*

One of the four *Mahāvākyas* is **अयं आत्मा ब्रह्म** *ayaṃ ātmā brahma.* That is, *ātman* is qualitatively the same as *Brahman.*

So, based on the unique capabilities of *Karma* and *Jñāna* bestowed on human beings, they can evolve to have a direct experience that they are the *ātman*, and not the body, not the mind, not the senses, but the witness of all these.

इदं पुच्छं प्रतिष्ठा। idaṃ puccham pratiṣṭhā [1.19]
इदं idaṃ - Here, पुच्छं puccham - in culmination (the hu-

man being is) प्रतिष्ठा pratiṣṭhā - consecrated (as the *Brahman*).

1.19 *Here, in culmination, the human being is consecrated as the Brahman.*

Thus, the cycle of creation is complete.

तदप्येष श्लोको भवति।

tadapyēṣaḥ śhlōkō bhavati [1.20]

The essence of knowledge and truth is described in a compact, poetic, and structured language.

Summary

The validity, in *ādhyātma vidhya* (spirituality), is established when one goes back to where one has started. Here, the essence of the *Upaniṣad* is so beautifully captured in just 20 lines.

The first line is a statement, "*The knower of Brahman attains the Supreme*" which inspires us to action: "*To achieve the Supreme bliss, one has to know the Brahman*".

The next 3 lines are the answer to "**Why this Creation?**"

The nature of *Brahman* as the *Sadchidānanda Swarūpa* is an irrefutable definition of the Ultimate Reality, which is termed as God. Through this, one knows God to be Omnipresent, Omniscient, and Omnipotent.

This *Brahman* is known through direct experience in the form of brilliant effulgence beyond the darkness of ignorance, within the inherent cave of *Buddhi*, which has been identified as the third ventricle that contains cerebrospinal fluid, at the center of the brain.

The *Brahmavid* (Knower), along with the *Brahman* (Known) enjoys all desires together with the all-knowing *Brahman*. This is alternatively explained as,

Inspired by the all-knowing Brahman, both Brahmavid and Brahman together have desired to become all that there is, this visible universe, so that they may enjoy together.

The next five lines describe "**How the process of Creation happened**" in concise form:

From the *ātman* (the very Self) has emerged *ākāśa*, the field of space that manifests the visible Universe.

From *Ākāśa* came forth *Vāyu*, the universal force, from which came *Agni* the thermo-nuclear fire, that gave rise to *Āpah*, the nuclear reaction processes, and finally, this paved the way to *Pṛthvī*, the formation of bonds, that gave rise to stable molecules.

The next five lines describe "**Evolution of Life on Earth**" figuratively:

From *Pṛthvī* has emerged the plant life (flora), which held the heat from the Sun's rays. The physical forms of various animals (Fauna) came forth from the plant life, which is their sustenance. Amongst these various combinations of physical forms arises *puruṣa*, the physical body of the human being. This has been hailed as the highest of all physical forms, as it is in this that nature achieved an appropriate ratio of 1:50 for the size of the brain to that of the body, which is found to be very effective and efficient in process of evolution.

The next five lines elucidate "**the purpose of human life**" at three different levels:

At the physical level, it describes the human being to be in the form of a bird, with a head, the right and left wings, a body at the center, and a supporting tail.

From a physiological perspective, the brain is seen to have the Cerebral Cortex as its head, the right and left hemispheres as its wings, the third ventricle as its center, and the medulla oblongata followed by the spinal column as its tail.

Philosophically, the human being is the only one who is endowed with the twin aspects of Karma and Jñāna, which can help them to have the direct experience of the luminous Self, to be their true nature.
Hence, at the end of Creation, the human being has been consecrated as Brahman, completing the cycle.

Thus, the purpose of Creation is summarised by Bhagavan Sri Sathya Sai Baba as
"**I have separated Myself from Myself so that I may love Myself**".

2

How to Know One Self

Introduction

The second part of *Brahmānanda Valli* is titled पञ्च-कोशः विवरणम्, "*pañcakōśha vivaraṇam*" meaning the exposition of the five sheaths or five layers on the Self. They represent the subtler layers that cover the Self and are key to understanding the inner methodology of self-inquiry. These five layers are, typically described as follows:

1. अन्नमयकोशः *Annamaya-kōśa*: The outermost sheath, associated with the physical gross body (*sthūla śarīra*), that is sustained by food and governs the processes of birth, growth, decay, and death.
2. प्राणमयकोशः *Prāṇamaya-kōśa*: The vital energy body composed of *prāṇa*, which governs the various physiological aspects such as respiratory, circulatory, excretory, digestive systems.
3. मनोमयकोशः *Manōmaya-kōśa*: The mind sheath, composed of *Manas* (thinking mind) consisting of emotions, desires, and thoughts as well as *Chitta*, memory aspect of the mind.
4. विज्ञानमयकोशः *Vijñānamaya-kōśa*: The intellect sheath consisting of the discriminating *Buddhi* assists in decision-making. It also involves *Ahaṃkāra* aspect, called as ego.
5. आनन्दमयकोशः *Ānandamaya-kōśa*: The Bliss sheath , consisting of Causal body (*kāraṇa śarīra*) is experienced in the aspects of happiness and deep sleep.

The three central layers of *prāṇamaya, manōmaya*, and *vijñānamaya*, constitute the subtle body (*sūkśma śarīra*). The 2nd to 6th *anuvākās* deal in detail about these five layers from gross to subtle and are established as the sheaths covering the Self but not the true Self.

In this book, it is postulated that these layers describe the process of refinement of the अन्तःकरण *antaḥkaraṇa*, literally "the inner instrument". It refers to the internal faculty through which the self (Ātman) experiences, perceives, and interacts with the world. The *antaḥkaraṇa* is not a physical organ, but a subtle, non-material apparatus. It is traditionally divided into four distinct but interconnected functions or parts.

1. मनस् *Manas*: It is the **Thinking mind** that consists of ***Sankalpa–Vikalpa*** forming and rejection of ideas.
2. बुद्धि *Buddhi*: It is the **Intellect** that consists of ***Nischaya***, that involves discrimination, decision-making and knowledge.
3. चित्त *Chitta* : It is the **Memory** that consists of ***Smaraṇa***, storage of impressions or *saṁskāras*, involves retention and recollection.
4. अहंकार *Ahaṅkāra*: It is the **ego**, that consists of ***Abhimāna***, sense of individuality and ownership, that involves **'I'-identity**.

Each *anuvāka* starts with the description of the various aspects of the layer or sheath under consideration. Then, it indicates the existence of an inner layer that fills the layer under consideration and has a form or nature similar to that of a human being. It finally ends with a description that is similar to that of the *puruṣa*, consisting of a head, two wings, a central body, and a supporting tail.

So, the second *anuvāka* starts with the description of the gross physical body, *annamaya kōśa*, which has already been referred to at the end of the first *anuvaka*, and leads us into the subtle layer of *prāṇamaya* within it and describes it.
Typically, the aspect of *Anna* or food is seen to be described in this paragraph. But, given the fact that one is talking about the human being, one must consider *annam*, a universal connotation of food, through all senses, to represent *annamaya śarīra* as before.

Annamaya Kōśa

अन्ना॒द्वै प्र॒जाः प्र॒जायंन्ते। याः काश्चंपृथि॒वीग्ं श्रि॒ताः।
अथो॒, अन्नेंनै॒व जींवन्ति। अथैंन॒दपिंयन्त्यन्त॒तः।

an'nādvaip' prajā[fp]' prajāyan'tē [2.1]
yā[ḥk]' kāśh'cha' pṛthivīgeśh' śhritā-ḥa [2.2]
atho, an'nēnaiva jīvan'ti [2.3]
athainadapi yan'tyan'tataḥa [2.4]

अन्नग्ं हि भूताना॒ं ज्येष्ठम्म्ं। तस्मा॑त् सर्वौष॒धमुंच्यते ।
सर्व॒ं वै तेऽन्नंमाप्नुवन्ति। येऽन्न॒ं ब्रह्मो॒पासंते।

an'nagmṁ' hi bhūtānāṁ' jyēṣh'ṭham'm [2.5]
tas'māāt' sar'vauṣhadhamuch'yatē [2.6]
sar'vaṁ' vai tē' (a)n'namāp'nuvan'ti [2.7]
yē' (a)n'naṁ' brah'mōpāsatē [2.8]

अन्नग्ं हि भूताना॒ं ज्येष्ठम्म्ं। तस्मा॑त् सर्वौष॒धमुंच्यते।
अन्नाॅद् भूतानि॒ जायंन्ते। जा ता॒न्यन्नेंन वर्धन्ते।
अद्यतेऽत्ति चं भूता॒नि। तस्मादन्नं तदुच्यंत, इ॒ति।

an'nagam hi bhūtānāṁ jyēṣṭham'm [2.9]
tas'māāt sar'vauṣhadhamuchyatē [2.10]
an'nāād bhūtāni jāyan'tē [2.11]
jātān'yan'nēna var'dhan'tē [2.12]
ad'yatē'tti cha bhūtāni [2.13]
tas'mādan'naṁ' taduch'yata, iti [2.14]

तस्माद्वा एतस्मादन्नंरस॒मयात्।
अन्योऽन्तर आत्माँप्राण॒मयः।
तेनैँष पू॒र्णः। स वा, एष पुरुषविंध, ए॒व।
तस्य पुरुंषवि॒धताम्। अन्वयँ पुरुष॒विधः ।

tas'mād'vā ētas'mādan'narasamayā-t [2.15]
an'yō'n'tara, ātmāap' prāṇamayaḥa [2.16]
tēnaiṣa pūrṇaḥa [2.17]
sa vā ēṣa puruṣavidha, ēva [2.18]
tasya puruṣavidhatām [2.19]
anvayaṁ puruṣhavidhaḥa [2.20]

तस्य प्राणंएव॒ शिरः। व्यानो दक्षिंणः प॒क्षः।
अपान उत्तंरः प॒क्षः। आकांश आ॒त्मा।
पृथिवी पुच्छ॒ं प्रति॒ष्ठा। तदप्येष श्लोंको भ॒वति।।

tas'yap' prāṇa eva śhiraḥa [2.21]
vyānō dak'ṣhiṇa[fp]' pak'ṣhaḥa [2.22]
apāna ut'tara[fp]' pakṣhaḥa [2.23] ākāśha ātmā [2.24]
pṛthivī puch'chhaṁ pratiṣh'ṭhā [2.25]
tadap'yēṣhash' śhlōkō bhavati [2.26]

Saṃsāra
The Cycle of Birth and Death

अन्नाद्वै प्रजाः प्रजायन्ते।

annādvai prajāḥ prajāyantē **[2.1]**

वै *vai* - Indeed, अन्नात् *annāt* - From food or from the physical form of the human being (outcome of food), who is the essence of *annamaya kōśas* (all available physical forms), प्रजाः *prajāḥ* - offspring (or beings) प्रजायन्ते *prajāyantē* - (of a similar kind) are born.

2.1 *From food, indeed, all beings are born.*
Indeed, from the physical form of a human being (an outcome of food), offspring (or beings of a similar kind) are born.

याः काश्च पृथ्वीग् श्रिताः।

yāḥ kāścha pṛthivīgeśritāḥ **[2.2]**

याः *yāḥ* - Those offspring, काश्च *kāścha* -whoever is born, श्रिताः *śritāḥ* - are also supported or take refuge on पृथ्वीग् *pṛthivīgṁ* - that which arises from Pṛthivī (Earth), that is the plant life (which is the basis for food).

2.2 *Whatever beings reside or 'take refuge' on Earth.*
Those offspring who are born are dependent on the plant life that arises from Earth for their food.

अथो अन्नेनैव जीवन्ति।

atho annēnaiva jīvanti [2.3]

अथो *atho* - Then, the physical forms thus born are अन्नेनैव *annēnaiva* - also sustained by food जीवन्ति *jīvanti* - to live.

2.3 *And they indeed live by food.*

Then, the physical forms that are born are also sustained by food to live.

अथैनदपि यन्त्यन्ततः। *athainadapi yantyantataḥ* [2.4]

अथैन *athaina* - Then, this (food) अपि *api* - also यन्ति *yanti* - they go अन्ततः *antataḥ* - at the very end.

2.4 *And, also into this (food), they go at the end.*

This can also be interpreted alternatively as follows:

अथैन athaina - Then, this अपि api - and so on (cycle) यन्ति yanti - goes अन्ततः antataḥ - till the very end.

2.4 Ultimately, these physical beings return to their food (Earth) form.

Then, this cycle is repeated again and again.

Summary

Indeed, from the physical form of human beings, who are an outcome of food, offspring are born. Those offspring who are born are dependent on the plant life that arises from Earth for their food. Then, the physical forms that are born are also sustained by food to live. Ultimately, these physical beings return to their food (Earth) form. This cycle is repeated again and again.

The Inner Journey to the Self

अन्नगं् हि भूतानां ज्येष्ठम्।

annagṃ hi bhūtānāṃ jyēṣṭham [2.5]

अन्नगं् *annagṃ* - Indeed, this physical form of human being (consisting of *annamaya*) sustained by food, हि *hi* - is indeed ज्येष्ठम् *jyēṣṭham* - the eldest or supreme भूतानां *bhūtānāṃ* - among the various living creatures or beings.

2.5 *Food is indeed the eldest (most venerable) of all beings.*
Indeed, the physical form of a human being is supreme among all beings.

तस्मात् सर्वौषधमुच्यते।

tasmāt sarvauṣadhamuchyatē [2.6]

उच्यते uchyatē - The exact meaning is 'said to be' or 'spoken of as'.
But, here the implied meaning from poetic sense can be taken as 'emerge out of' just as spoken word emerges from the mouth.
तस्मात् *tasmāt* - Hence सर्व *sarva* - all (living beings) उच्यते *uchyatē* - are said to (emerge from) औषधि *ouṣhadhi* - the plant life (which is the basis for food). This is also referred to as medicine.

2.6 *Therefore, food is called the universal medicine.* Hence, all living beings are said to emerge from the plant life, which is the basis for food.

सर्वं वै तेऽन्नमाप्नुवन्ति।

sarvaṁ vai tē'nnamāpnuvanti [2.7]

सर्वं *sarvaṃ* - Everything or All वै *vai* - indeed आप्नुवन्ति *āpnuvanti* - is attained ते *tē* - by that अन्नम् *annam* - physical form (of human being), its simple meaning is food.

2.7 *All indeed, they attain, as food.*

Everything is attained by that physical form of human being. Why?

येऽन्नं ब्रह्मोपासते।

yē'nnaṁ brahmōpāsatē [2.8]

ये *yē* - Those अन्नम् *annaṁ* - human beings with physical form उपासते *upāsatē* - worship or meditate upon ब्रह्म *brahma* - *Brahman*, the Ultimate Reality.

2.8 *Those who meditate on* Brahman *as food, they attain everything (as food).*

Those human beings, with the physical form, worship or meditate upon *Brahman.* Once they meditate upon the ultimate reality, they are on the path to cross over the cycle of birth and death. So, the rest of the verses, even though they are a repetition of previous verses, take on a deeper meaning.

अन्नगं् हि भूतानां ज्येष्ठम्।

annagam hi bhūtānāṁ jyēṣṭham [2.9]

अन्नगं् *annagam* - This physical form of the human being (consisting of *annamaya*) हि *hi* - is indeed ज्येष्ठम् *jyēṣṭham* - the eldest or supreme भूतानां *bhūtānāṁ* - among the various living creatures or beings.

2.9 ***Food is indeed the eldest of all beings.***
Since human beings meditate upon Brahman, they are supreme among all beings.

तस्मात् सर्वौषधमुच्यते॥
tasmāt sarvauṣadhamuchyatē **[2.10]**

तस्मात् *tasmāt* - Hence सर्व *sarva* - for all (ailments) उच्यते *uchyatē* - is said to be औषधि *ouṣhadhi* - medicine/remedy.

2.10 ***Therefore, it (food) is called "the universal medicine".***
Hence, it is said, the physical form of human beings, meditating upon Brahman, is the remedy for all ailments. Philosophically, the only ailment one is suffering from is the *Saṃsāra*, the cycle of birth and death.

अन्नाद् भूतानि जायन्ते।
annād bhūtāni jāyantē **[2.11]**

अन्नाद् *annād* - From food, भूतानि *bhūtāni* - beings जायन्ते *jāyantē* - are born (originatē).

2.11 ***From food, beings are born.***
Here, food should not be limited to only that which is taken through the mouth. Food is that which is taken in through all the senses. Such food shapes our thoughts and behaviour. So, it constantly gives birth to a new person.

जातान्यन्नेन वर्धन्ते।

jātānyannēna vardhantē [2.12]

जातानि *jātāni* - Those human beings that are born अन्नेन *annēna* - from the food (taken through various senses) वर्धन्ते *vardhantē* - continue to grow.

2.12 *Once born, they grow by food.*

Those human beings that are born from the food through various senses continue to grow (in knowledge) as they seek the ultimate reality.

अद्यतेऽत्ति च् भूतानि।

adyatē'tti cha bhūtāni [2.13]

च् *cha* - And भूतानि *bhūtāni* - these human beings अत्ति *a'tti* - are consumed ते *te'* - by that अद्यते *adyatē* - which they consume.

2.13 *It (food) is eaten, and it (food) eats beings. "The eater becomes the eaten", indicating a cyclic nature.*

These human beings are consumed by what they consume. Philosophically, one is completely consumed by that which they consume: यद्भावं तत्भवति *"yad bhāvam tat bhavati"* - *"As one thinks or feels, so one becomes"* or *"Whatever the state of being, that it becomes."*

तस्मादन्नं तदुच्यत इति।

tasmādannaṁ taduchyata iti [2.14]

तस्मात् *tasmāt* - Hence, everything उच्यत *uchyata* - is said to be (emerges) तद् *tad* - from that अन्नम् *annaṁ* - food,

इति *iti* - for sure.

2.14 *Hence, it is said that everything is from that food.*

Hence, all progress is said to be from food, consumed through various senses by human beings, for sure.

Summary

All living beings are said to emerge from the plant life. The physical form of the human being is indeed supreme among all the physical forms of living beings. Everything is attained by the physical form of a human being, who worships or meditates upon the Brahman.

Since human beings meditate upon Brahman, they are supreme among all beings. Hence, it is said, the physical form of human beings is the remedy for all ailments. Philosophically, the only ailment one is suffering from is the ***Saṃsāra****, the cycle of birth and death. Food is that which is taken in through all the senses. Such food shapes our thoughts and behaviour. So, it constantly gives birth to a new person. Those who are thus born, through constant inputs from various senses, continue to grow in their journey towards Brahman.*

These human beings are consumed by what they consume. "yad bhāvam tat bhavati" (यद्भावं तत्भवति): "As one thinks or feels, so one becomes" or whatever the state of being, that it becomes. Hence, all progress is said to be from food, consumed through various senses by human beings, for sure.

Identification of *Prāṇamaya Śarīra*

One slowly becomes aware of an inner self, governed by the vital breath as one meditates.

तस्माद्वा एतस्मादन्नरसमयात्।
tasmādvā ētasmādannarasamayāt **[2.15]**

तस्मात् *tasmāt* + वा *vā* - Therefore, from that very (physical form) एतस्माद *ētasmād* - this रस *rasa* - essence of अन्नमयात् *annamayāt* - physical forms (of human beings) emerge.

2.15 *Therefore, from this (self) consisting of the essence of food* ...
Therefore, from that very physical form, which is the essence of all physical forms, emerges this ...

अन्योऽन्तर आत्मा प्राणमयः।
anyo'ntara ātmā prāṇamayaḥ **[2.16]**

अन्यः *anyaḥ* - Another अन्तर *antara* - inner आत्मा *ātmā* - self (of human being) प्राणमयः *prāṇamayaḥ* - filled with prāṇa or vital breath.

2.16 ... ***There is another inner self made of prāṇa (vital breath).***
... another inner Self of a human being, which is filled with *prāṇa* (vital breath).

तेनैष पूर्णः। *tēnaiṣa pūrṇaḥ* **[2.17]**

तेन *tēna* - By that (vital breath or *prāṇa*) एषः *ēṣaḥ* - this (physical form of human being) पूर्णः *pūrṇaḥ* - is completely filled with.

2.17 *By that (prāṇamaya), this (annamaya) is filled or made complete.*

स वा एष पुरुषविध एव।

sa vā ēṣa puruṣavidha ēva [**2.18**]

सः *sa* - That (*prāṇa* or vital breath) वा *vā* - verily has एष *ēṣa* - this पुरुषविधः *puruṣavidhaḥ* - form of *puruṣa* (human being) एव *ēva* - itself.

2.18 *Indeed, this (prāṇamaya self) is in the form of a person.*
That *prāṇamaya* self verily has this form of human being itself and is of the same nature.

तस्य पुरुषविधताम्।

tasya puruṣavidhatām [**2.19**]

तस्य *tasya* - That *prāṇamaya* self पुरुषविधताम् *puruṣavid-hatām* - has the likeness of the form of a human being.

2.19 "*Its form is like that of a person.*"
That *prāṇamaya* self is similar to the form of a human being.

अन्वयं पुरुषविधः।

anvayaṁ puruṣavidhaḥ [**2.20**]

अन्वयं *anvayaṃ* - Correspondence पुरुषविधः *puruṣavidhaḥ* - similar to that of *puruṣa*.

2.20 *In correspondence to the form of a human being, as described before.*

Summary

Therefore, from that very physical form of human being, which is the essence of all physical forms, emerges another inner self of human being, which is filled with prāṇa (vital breath). By that (prāṇamaya), this (annamaya) is filled or made complete.
That vital energy has the very form of the human being itself and is of the same nature.
Here, is the description of prāṇa, in correspondence to the form of a human being, as described before.

Description of *Prāṇamaya Śarīra*

तस्य प्राण एव शिरः। *tasya prāṇa ēva śiraḥ* [2.21]

2.21 ***It has Prāṇa as its head.***

व्यानो दक्षिणः पक्षः। *vyānō dakṣiṇaḥ pakṣaḥ*[2.22]

2.22 ***Vyāna is its right side.***

अपान उत्तरः पक्षः। *apāna uttaraḥ pakṣaḥ* [2.23]

2.23 ***Apāna is its left side.***

आकाश आत्मा। *ākāśa ātmā* [2.24]

2.24 ***Ākāśa as center.***

पृथिवी पुच्छं प्रतिष्ठा। *pṛthivī puccham̐ pratiṣṭhā* [2.25]

2.25 ***Pṛthivī is the tail, established as the support.***

This description of *prāṇa*, which mentions *ākāśa* and *pṛthivī*, was very surprising. One would have expected *samāna* and *udāna vāyus* instead. The idea to consider *śiraḥ*, etc., as adjectives alongside nouns was revisited. *Prāṇa*, the vital energy, indeed is the highest (*śiraḥ*) form of food. *Vyāna* is the working aspect (*dakṣiṇaḥ*) that distributes energy to the entire body, and *Apāna* is responsible for the downward flow of energy, which assists in elimination as well as childbirth, a higher aspect (*uttara*). Then, what is the central aspect of vital energy that is represented by *ākāśa*? And, what does *pṛthivī* signify as culmination (*puccham̐*) or end?

This reminded me of Swami mentioning that the *bṛhu-*

madhya sthāna, the area between the two eyebrows, is representative of *ākāśa*, the mind space. Since *pṛthivī* symbolises stability or steadiness, it occurred to me that the description is intended to achieve stability of mind. **This is the key insight that inspired me to write this book.**

तदप्येष श्लोंको भवति।

tadapyēṣa śhlōkō bhavati [2.26]

2.26 The essence of knowledge and truth is described in a compact, poetic, and structured language.

Physiological Perspective of *Prāṇamaya Śarīra:*

***Prāṇa Vāyu* (*Śiraḥ* or Head):** It is a process of inhalation or intake of vital energy that supports the respiratory system, spinal cord, and head. This results in sensory perception and mental clarity.

***Vyāna Vāyu* (*Dakṣatā* or Working Aspect):** This is the vital energy that supports the blood circulatory system in the distribution of energy and nutrition to all parts of the body.

***Apāna Vāyu* (*Uttara* or Higher Aspect):** This is the vital energy that supports the process of elimination in the excretory system and reproduction. It resides in the pelvic region.

***Samāna Vāyu* (*Ātman* or Central Aspect):** This is the vital energy that supports the digestive system and resides near the navel in the abdominal region (center of body). It helps in the accumulation of energy derived from food and its distribution.

***Udāna Vāyu* (*Puccham̐* or Tail):** This is the vital energy that supports the nervous system through its upward moment from the throat to the head. It can be seen as the energy responsible for expressing thoughts articulated into words through the throat and mouth. As it counters the *prāṇa vāyu*, the head of the *prāṇa* body, and stabilizes it, it may be considered as the tail. Typically, *samāna* and *udāna vāyus* have been interpreted to represent the *ākāśa* and *pṛthvī*, respectively.

Philosophical Perspective of *Prāṇamaya Śarīra:*

Prāṇa is the highest energy channelling through the सुषुम्णा नाडी *Suṣumṇā Nāḍī* [16], meaning the very gracious or the most pleasant channel. It is the spiritual axis of the subtle body, running from the base of the spine to the crown of the head. It is the primary path for knowledge and the energy responsible for spiritual awakening.

Vyāna can be taken as representative of the energy through the right channel called पिङ्गला *Piṅgalā Nāḍī*. It is responsible for stimulating energy linked to the sympathetic nervous system and influences activity and outward focus.

Apāna can be taken as representative of the energy through the left channel, called इडा *Iḍā Nāḍī*. It is responsible for cooling and calming energy, and is linked to the parasympathetic nervous system, influencing relaxation and introspection.

Meerabai, a great devotee of Lord Krishna sang about the channeling of these three energies as follows:

चलो रे मन गंगा यमुना तीर।

chalo re man gangā yamunā tīr

"Oh Mind! Let's go to the Sangam (meeting place between the eyebrows) of Ganga (vital energy flow through left nostril) and Yamuna (vital energy flow through right nostril)".

Sandhya Vandanam

During *Sandhya Vandanam*, that is, a prayerful meditation before the break of dawn or at dusk (*Sandhya*), one sits in *Āsana* (स्थिरं सुखम् आसनम् ; *sthiraṃ sukham āsanam*), that which is steady and comfortable, in front of one's altar by lighting a lamp. The process requires cleansing oneself and avoiding distractions by choosing a quiet and clean place.

Importance of *Āsana*: If a vessel is not steady, then the water cannot remain still. Similarly, if the body is not still, then the mind also will be unsteady.

Importance of *Pratyāhara* (withdrawal of senses):

Sitting in a quiet, clean corner reduces the inputs to the senses, thereby making their withdrawal from outward sensations easier. This helps in concentrating the mind.

Normally, the *prāṇa* flows through *Iḍā* and *Piṅgalā*, alternating dominance, and rarely through *Suṣumṇā* [16]. *Suṣumṇā* becomes active when breath through both nostrils flows equally; this is a sign of *prāṇa* in balance.

अनुलोम-विलोम *anulōma-vilōma prāṇāyāma*: This is done for purifying the left and right channels and balancing them.

- **अनुलोम *anulōma*:** Inhalation through the left nostril by keeping the right nostril closed.
- **विलोम *vilōma*:** Exhaling through the right nostril by closing the left nostril.
- **अनुलोम *anulōma*:** Inhalation through the right nostril while holding the left nostril closed.
- **विलोम *vilōma*:** Exhaling through the left nostril by closing the right nostril.

The above procedure is repeated 11 or 21 times.
When *Iḍā* and *Piṅgalā* are thus balanced, the *prāṇa* is directed into *Suṣumṇā*. Then, *prāṇāyāma* is practised.

To emphasise the importance of prāṇayama, here is a small story.

A Small Story:

Once there lived a king whose subjects were very happy, and the kingdom was very prosperous. One year, due to lack of rains, the crop failed, and people were subject to difficulties. The king helped them with grains from his granary. Unfortunately, the situation was similar in the next year, and the king had distributed the grains meant for a war-like situation to his people. Then, the king reflected that, if this continued for another year, his subjects would be in great danger. So, he went to the temple and prayed to the Lord sincerely for the emancipation of the suffering of his people. Lord, out of compassion, appears to the king and gives him a Genie, a magical creature that can do anything for the king, with a condition: "If the Genie is not given any work, it would devour the king."

The king put the Genie to work and got a lot of wells and ponds dug. Fortunately, the rains arrived next year, and the ponds and reservoirs filled. Then, he utilised the Genie to make roads, houses, and also got security built for his kingdom. In a few years, the kingdom was more prosperous than ever, and all the subjects were happy. The king is now faced with the danger of being devoured by the Genie, as there is no work to be given to it. He goes back again to the temple and prays to the Lord for a solution to the new problem that he is faced with. The Lord, out of mercy, appeared and told the king: "Oh!

King! You have such a large garden in your courtyard. Place a pole in the middle and ask the Genie to go up and down the pole till you need it to perform a new task." The king is overjoyed at the simple solution and places his gratitude at the Lord's feet.

All of us are gifted with a mind, a Genie, that can accomplish very daunting tasks; if it is left idle, it can drive one insane. The way to avoid the idle mind is through the process of *prāṇayāma*, where one focuses on the incoming and outgoing breath, concentrating on the *ākāśa sthāna*, the region between the eyebrows.

What does *ākāśa* represent within us?

It is the mind-space that is filled with *sankalpas* (intentions) to perform various tasks.

What does *Pṛthvī* signify?

It represents the stability or steadiness of the mind-space referred to as *manas*.

How does this steadiness get established, and why is it necessary?

Personal Experience

It was at the end of our third year undergraduate program at Brindavan, Bhagawan Sri Sathya Sai Baba's ashram at Whitefield, Bengaluru. His followers address Bhagawan as Swami, which translates to master or mentor. All of us students from the final year of undergraduate studies prayed for an opportunity to get a special interaction with Swami inside His residence, named *Trayee Brindavan*, exclusively for our batch, so that we could offer our gratitude. I took this opportunity to prepare a greeting card, expressing our gratitude, to Swami. On a Sunday, all of us were seated in *Trayee*, with prayers in our hearts, eagerly awaiting His Divine Direction. By His Divine Grace, I got the opportunity to sit close and offer the gratitude card into His hands. Swami opened the card and read the poem written inside:

This is all I ask

Lord! Show me the way
I can somehow repay
The blessings You have given to me ...
Lord! Teach me to do
what You much want me to
And to be what You want me to be ...
I am certainly unworthy, I know
But I do Love You so
I beg You to answer my plea ...
I have not much to give
But as long as I live
May I give myself completely to Thee!

Swami read the whole poem and then read it again and stopped at the line '**What You much want me to do**' and read it out loud and said, *"I want you to do only one thing:* ***Less talk, More study****".* Then, Swami added,

"Not only this boy, but from all of you, I want that you follow this simple dictum: "Less talk, more study".

Swami then blessed all of us with His Discourse and accepted our offerings. These sweet memories filled our lives and have sanctified our existence, for which we will ever remain grateful to *Swami*.

At that point in time, being students, we had taken the message to be: We should concentrate on our studies and reduce talking. For *Swami* said that, when we talk less, automatically we reduce many bad habits like lying, criticising and making fun of others, idle gossip, and other such negative pursuits.

Later, on reflection, it dawned that *Swami* had said, "Less Talk, More Study" and not "Talk Less, Study More". This changed the perspective. 'Less talk' means reducing chatter in your mind-space. This is possible when we reduce *sankalpas* that arise due to excessive desires and attachments. *Swami* often said in His discourses, ***"Study for Steady"***. In other words, one must study one's mind, observe the thoughts and intentions that arise there, and slowly discard those that are not necessary for spiritual progress. Gradually, the distracting chatter and unsteadiness of the mind reduce, and a calm follows, increasing concentration or focus during meditation.

The next question is, why does one need steadiness?

How to see one's own face?

Rarely do we realize that one cannot see one's own face.

What do we need to see our own face?
Obviously, the first thought is a mirror (or our own mobile camera in selfie mode!). In ancient times, it would have been a pond of water.
Even though it seems obvious and a simple task to see one's reflection, it actually requires many conditions to be met.

The mirror (pond) should be steady. If the mirror (pond) is constantly moving, one can hardly see one's face clearly.

Even if the mirror were steady, but there were no lights, no image would be visible in the mirror. Hence, **one needs illumination**.

Assuming the mirror is steady, and there is illumination, one needs **the mirror to be clean and pure**.

Given that the above three conditions are met: the mirror is steady, clean, and there is illumination; one still cannot see one's face, unless **one has eyes and is alive**. That is, the *Prajñā Śakti*, the life force responsible for the senses to function, needs to be recognized, and one should always be aware of it. We most often take this obvious aspect for granted.

To summarise, to be able to see a reflection of one's own face,

1. The mirror/pond has to be steady (Stable)
2. The mirror/pond and face to be illuminated (Lit up)
3. The mirror/pond to be pure (Clean)
4. The person has to be alive with open working eyes (Aware).

Now, typically, when one sees one's own face, one feels extremely happy, and naturally, one smiles.

What would be the level of happiness when one sees one's own true self?
It is called **Bliss or *Ānanda***.
Let us delve into understanding the *pañcakōśha vivaraṇam* (description of the five sheaths) of *Brahmānanda Valli* from the perspective of the mind acting as a mirror by comprehending its four aspects of *manas, buddhi, chitta*, and *ahaṃkāra*, as the four conditions that need to be met.

Summary

Prāṇa, indeed, is the (*śiraḥ*) highest form of food. It energizes the *Suṣumṇā Nāḍī.*

Vyāna as *dakṣiṇaḥ pakṣaḥ*: Considering *dakṣiṇaḥ*, as an adjective, *Vyāna* is the working aspect that distributes energy through all *nāḍīs*. When considered to be a noun, it is along the right side of the body and can be considered to represent *Pingala Nāḍī*, which influences the sympathetic nervous system responsible for activities and outward focus.

Apāna, as *uttara pakṣaḥ*: Considering *uttara*, as an adjective, *Apāna* is higher aspect that is responsible for childbirth and when taken to be a noun, it is along the left side of the body and can be considered to represent the *Iḍā Nāḍī*, which governs the parasympathetic nervous system responsible for introspection and leads to relaxation.

When *Vyāna* and *Apāna* are balanced, the spiritual energy flows through the *Suṣumṇā Nāḍī*, the central energy channel that leads to the realisation ***ākāśa ātma***. It reflects the ultimate truth that, "*ātman* is *ākāśa* (self-luminous)".

Thus, the ***prāṇamaya* body is consecrated**, in the end, and is established as the *pṛthivī tattwam*, which represents the attainment of **steadiness of the mind**.

Hence, in the inward journey, the first aspect is the mastery of the constantly thinking mind by achieving steadiness, a representation of "*pṛthvī tattwam*". Considering the mind as a mirror, it is interesting to observe that steadiness is a reflection of *pṛthivī* (See cover page).

Prāṇamaya Kōśa

प्राणं देवा, अनुप्राणंन्ति। मनुष्याः पशवंश्च ये।
प्राणो हि भूतानामायुः। तस्मांत् सर्वायुषमुंच्यते।
सर्वंमेव त, आयुंर्यन्ति। ये प्राणं ब्रह्मोपासंते।
प्राणो हि भूतांनामायुः। तस्मात् सर्वायुषमुच्यंत, इति।

prāṇaṁ' dēvā, anuprāṇan'ti [3.1]
manuṣhyāa[fp]' paśhavaśhcha yē [3.2]
prāṇō hi bhūtānāmāyuḥu [3.3]
tas'māat' sar'vāyuṣhamuch'yatē [3.4]
sar'vamēva ta, āyur'yan'ti [3.5]
yēp' prāṇaṁ' brah'mōpāsatē [3.6]
prāṇō hi bhūtānāmāyuḥu [3.7]
tas'māt' sar'vāyuṣhamuch'yata, iti [3.8]

तस्यैष एव शारींर आत्मा। यः पूर्वस्य।
तस्माद्वा एतस्मांत्प्राणमयात्।
अन्योऽन्तर, आत्मां मनोमयः।
तेनैंष पूर्णः। स वा एष पुरुषविंध, एव।
तस्य पुरुंषविधताम्। अन्वयं पुरुषविधः।

tas'yaiṣha, ēva śhārīra, ātmā [3.9]
ya[fp]' pur'vasya [3.10]
tas'mād'vā, ētas'māatprāṇamayā-t [3.11]
an'yōn'tara, ātmā manōmayaḥa [3.12]
tēnaiṣha pūrṇaḥa [3.13]
sa vā, ēṣha puruṣhavidha, ēva [3.14]
tas'ya puruṣhavidhatām [3.15]

an'vayaṁ puruṣhavidhaḥa [3.16]

तस्य यजुरेव शिरः। ऋग्दक्षिणः पक्षः।
सामोत्तरः पक्षः। आदेश, आत्मा।
अथर्वाङ्गिरसः पुच्छं प्रतिष्ठा। तदप्येष श्लोको भवति॥

tas'ya yajurēva śhiraḥa [3.17],
ṛg'dak'ṣhiṇa[fp]' pakṣhaḥa [3.18]
sāmōt'tara[fp]' pak'ṣhaḥa [3.19],
ādēśha, ātmā [3.20]
athar'vāṅ'girasa[fp]' puch'chhaṁ' pratiṣh'ṭhā [3.21]
tadap'yēṣhash' śhlōkō bhavati| [3.22]

Life as Breath Cycle

प्राणं देवा अनु प्राणन्ति। मनुष्याः पशवश्च ये।
***prāṇaṁ dēvā anu prāṇanti* [3.1],**
***manuṣyāḥ paśavaścha yē* [3.2]**

प्राणं *prāṇaṃ* - vital breath देवा *dēvā* - is derived from the dēvas (divine light or radiation) अनु *anu* - and thereafter it sustains मनुष्याः *manuṣyāḥ* - human beings पशवश्च ये *paśavaścha yē* - and animals, birds, etc.

3.1, 3.2 *The vital breath is derived from radiation, and thereafter it sustains the human beings and animals, birds, etc.*

An alternative meaning can be considered by interpreting *dēvas* as sense organs (or इन्द्रियम् *indriyam*) because *Indra* is the King (Master) of *dēvas*. Conceptually, *Indra*

(इन्द्रियों के अधिपति *indriyoṃ ke adhipati*) is the controller (or Master) of the *Indriyas* (sense organs), which is the mind.

प्राणं *prāṇaṃ* - vital breath energises देवा *dēvā* - sense organs अनु *anu* - and thereafter it sustains (the sense organs of) मनुष्याः *manuṣyāḥ* - human beings पशवश्च ये *paśavaścha yē* - and those of animals, birds etc.

3.1, 3.2 *The sense organs are sustained by the vital breath in human beings, animals, birds, etc.*

प्राणो हि भूतानामायुः।

prāṇo hi bhūtānāmāyuḥ **[3.3]**

प्राणः *prāṇaḥ* - vital breath हि *hi* - is indeed responsible for आयुः *āyuḥ* - life (or their lifespan) भूतानाम *bhūtānām* - in all living beings.

3.3 *The balance or flow of vital breath within the body directly influences one's longevity and vitality.*

तस्मात् सर्वायुषमुच्यते।

tasmāt sarvāyuṣamuchyatē **[3.4]**

तस्मात् *tasmāt* - Hence, सर्व *sarva* - all (living beings) उच्यते *uchyatē* - are said to आयुषम् *āyuṣam* - have a lifespan (with *prāṇa* as the basis).

3.4 *Hence, all living beings are said to have a life span with prāṇa as the basis.*

सर्वमेव त आयुर्यन्ति। ***sarvamēva ta āyuryanti*** **[3.5]**

सर्वमेव *sarvamēva* - Everything, indeed त *ta* - which has आयुर्यन्ति *āyuryanti* - a lifespan moves towards it (prāṇa)

3.5 *Everything, which has a lifespan, indeed moves towards it.*

ये प्राणं ब्रह्मोपासते।

yē prāṇaṁ brahmōpāsatē **[3.6]**

ये *yē* - Those प्राणं *prāṇam* - living beings ब्रह्मोपासते *brahmōpāsatē* - worship or meditate upon the Brahman.

3.6 *Those who worship or meditate upon the Brahman as prāṇa.*

Those living beings, who are sustained by the vital breath, worship or meditate upon the Brahman.

प्राणो हि भूतानामायुः।

prāṇō hi bhūtānāmāyuḥ **[3.7]**

प्राण: *prāṇaḥ* - The vital breath हि *hi* - is indeed responsible for आयु: *āyuḥ* - life भूतानाम *bhūtānām* - in all living beings.

3.7 *The vital breath is indeed responsible for life in all living beings.*

Indeed, human beings come alive by focusing on this *prāṇa*, the vital breath. Human beings truly awaken to life when they become aware of *prāṇa*, or center their attention on it. As they meditate, they gain control over their Prāṇa and achieve steadiness of their mind.

तस्मात् सर्वायुषमुच्यत इति।

tasmāt sarvāyuṣamuchyata iti **[3.8]**

तस्मात् *tasmāt* - Hence, सर्व *sarva* - everything उच्यते *uchyate* - is said to be आयुषम् *āyuṣam* - (filled with) life.

3.8 *Hence, it (prāṇa) is said to be that which sustains the life of all beings. Prāṇa is the common thread of existence in all beings.*

That is, for those who worship Brahman, everything comes alive. They become full of life, both literally and metaphorically.

Summary

The vital breath that is responsible for life, in human beings, animals, and birds, etc., is derived from radiation and is sustained by it. This vital breath, transmuted into energy, energises the sense organs in all living beings. It is indeed responsible for the lifespan in all living beings. Hence, all living beings are said to have a lifespan, and everything that has a lifespan indeed moves toward prāṇa. Those living beings, sustained by prāṇa, worship or meditate upon the Brahman.

Human beings truly awaken to life when they become aware of prāṇa, and center their attention on it. As they meditate, they gain control over their Prāṇa and achieve steadiness of their mind. For those who worship Brahman, everything comes alive. They become full of life.

Identification of an Inner Self

तस्यैष एव शारीर आत्मा। यः पूर्वस्य।

***tasyaiṣa ēva śārīra ātmā* [3.9]**

***yaḥ pūrvasya* [3.10]**

तस्य *tasya* - Of that (talking of which) एषः *ēṣaḥ* - this (prāṇa) एव *ēva* - is indeed शारीर आत्मा *śārīra ātmā* - the embodied self यः *yaḥ* - who is पूर्वस्य *pūrvasya* - of the former (*annamaya* body).

3.9, 3.10 *This, the prāṇamaya kōśa, is indeed the embodied self (śārīra ātmā) of the previous, the annamaya kōśa.*

This prāṇa is indeed the very self of the physical body.

Prāṇa is the subtlest of the food that sustains the body. One can sustain the lifespan of one's body by living on breath alone.

Example: Lakshmanā in Rāmayana sustained his life without eating anything for 14 years during the *vanavāsā* (their life residing in the forest).

तस्माद्वा एतस्मात्प्राणमयात्।

***tasmādvā ētasmāt prāṇamayāt* [3.11]**

तस्माद्वा *tasmādvā* - From that, indeed एतस्मात् *ētasmāt* - from this very प्राणमयात् *prāṇamayāt* - (sheath) consisting of *prāṇa.*

3.11 *From that, indeed, from this very sheath consisting of prāṇamaya is ...*

अन्योऽन्तर आत्मा मनोमयः।

anyo'ntara ātmā manōmayaḥ [3.12]

अन्यः *anyaḥ* - Another अन्तर *antara* - inner आत्मा *ātmā* - self मनोमयः *manōmayaḥ* - filled with mind).

3.12 *...another inner self that is filled with mind.* The mind is comprised of a bundle of thoughts that are always doubting and questioning. It has a highly wavering nature. It is very powerful because of **three sakthis:**
Icchā Sakthi (the power of desire or will),
Jñāna Sakthi (the power to make decisions based on knowledge), and
Kriyā Sakthi (the power to motivate action).

तेनैष पूर्णः।

tēnaiṣa pūrṇaḥ [3.13]

तेन *tena* - By that (mind) एषः *ēṣaḥ* - this (*prāṇa*) पूर्णः *pūrṇaḥ* - is complete or full of.

3.13 *Just as the entire physical form is filled with prāṇa, so also, the entire prāṇa form is filled with mind.*

स वा एष पुरुषविध एव।

sa vā ēṣa puruṣavidha ēva [3.14]

स *sa* - That (mind) वा *vā* - verily has एष *ēṣa* - this पुरुषविध *puruṣavidha* - form of *puruṣa* एव *ēva* - itself.

3.14 *That mind, verily, has this form of the human being itself.*

This mind, verily, has a form similar to that of a human being itself and not different from it.

तस्य पुरुषविधताम्।

tasya puruṣavidhatām **[3.15]**

तस्य *tasya* - That (mind) पुरुषविधताम् *puruṣavidhatām* - has likeness of the form or nature of *puruṣa* being described.

3.15 ***That mind has the likeness of the form of a human being.***

अन्वयं पुरुषविधः।

anvayaṁ puruṣavidhaḥ **[3.16]**

अन्वयं *anvayaṃ* - Here is the description of the mind corresponding to पुरुषविधः *puruṣavidhaḥ* - the form or nature of *puruṣa* (human being).

3.16 ***Here is the description of the mind corresponding to the form of the human being.***

Summary

There is another inner layer comprising the mind with which the vital sheath is filled. Just as the entire physical form is filled with prāṇa, so also, the entire prāṇa form is filled with mind. This mind has verily a form similar to that of a human being itself, and its description is similar to that of puruṣa.

Description of *Manōmaya Śarīra*

तस्य यजुरेव शिरः। *tasya yajurēva śiraḥ* [3.17]

3.17 ***It has Yajurvēda as its head***

ऋग्दक्षिणः पक्षः। *ṛgdakṣiṇaḥ pakṣaḥ* [3.18]

3.18 ***The Rigvēda is its right arm***

सामोत्तरः पक्षः। sāmottaraḥ pakṣaḥ [3.19]

3.19 ***The Samavēda is its left arm***

आदेश आत्मा। | *ādēśa ātmā* [3.20]

3.20 ***It's self or central aspect is Ādēśa***

अथर्वाङ्गिरसः पुच्छं प्रतिष्ठा।
atharvāṅgīrasaḥ puccham̐ pratiṣṭhā [3.21]

3.21 ***Atharva and Aṅgīrasa are lower members on which it rests abidingly.***

Here, *Yajur* is considered the highest. The root word *yaj* means to sacrifice. **What should one sacrifice?**

One has to sacrifice the untruth, that is, *anātma bhāva*, the feelings related to non-self, such as *dēha bhāva* (body consciousness). The highest form of *prāṇa* is the pure thought of *ātman*. *Swami* said, आलोचना *ālochana* is *ātma lochana*, that is, the thought fixed in the *ātman*.

The *riks* are mantrās, which are often repeated, the working aspect (*dakṣiṇaḥ*). The basic definition of mantra is मननात् त्रायते इति मंत्रः "*Mananāt trāyatē iti mantrāh*".

मननात् *Mananāt* - constant repetition; त्रायते *Trāyatē* - to liberate; इति *Iti* - thus.

Thus, mantrās are those which are constantly repeated to attain liberation, which is a state of illumination.

Sāma is an equal-mindedness resulting in tranquillity, a higher (*uttara*) state of mind.

Ādēśa has been extensively analysed [17] to mean 'an indication'. So '*ādēśa ātma*' clearly connotes '**an indication to the self**' by the seeker.

Philosophical Perspective of Manōmaya Śarīra:

Yajurvēda, that represents ***Karma-kanda*** of the *vēdas*, is considered the head of the mind-body complex. It requires one to practice *yajña* or sacrifice (not necessarily literally) at all times.

The inner significance of *yajña* is to sacrifice the untruth so that the Truth shines forth, in consonance with the prayer: **असतो मा सद्गमय।** ***asato mā sadgamaya***
Lead us from untruth to Truth.

Rigvēda, that represents ***Jñāna-kanda*** of the *vēdas*, is the *dakṣiṇaḥ pakṣaḥ*, which involves the reasoning capabilities that lead to knowledge by dispelling the darkness of ignorance. This resonates with the prayer:
तमसो मा ज्योतिर्गमय। ***tamaso mā jyotirgamaya***
Lead us from darkness of ignorance to Light.

Samavēda, that represents the ***Upāsanā-kāṇḍa*** of the *vēdas*, is the *uttara pakṣaḥ*, which involves raising the level of consciousness, thereby leading to the immortal state of Oneness. This is attuned with the prayer:

मृत्योर्मा अमृतं गमय॥ mṛtyor mā amṛtaṁgamaya
Lead us from death to Immortality.

Ādēśa is considered as an indication [17] from the Guru. Hence, *Ādēśa* can be considered as *Gurōpadeshaṁ.*

During the *Upanayana Saṁskāra*, the sacred thread ceremony, which is performed after one reaches the age of seven, the *Guru* or Father gives the *Upadēśa* in the form of *Gāyatrī Mantra.*

Ādēśa, as said above, is an indication by the *Guru* and can be construed as *Gurōpadēsham.* There is a beautiful episode, concerning this, in *Shirdi Sai Satcharita* [18] wherein *Shirdi Baba* explains to his devotee Nanashaheb the true meaning of a *Gita śhlōka* (BG-4.34) [19].

An Episode:

Once, Nanasaheb was performing *pādasēva*, massaging his *Guru*'s feet, and murmuring to himself a particular *śhlōka* from the *Bhagavad Gita.* Then the following conversation ensued:

Shirdi Baba: What are you murmuring Nana?
Nana: Baba! I am chanting *Bhagavad Gita śhlōka.*
Baba: Let me listen to it.

Nana:

तद्विद्धि प्रणिपातेन परिप्रश्नेन सेवया ।
उपदेक्ष्यन्ति ते ज्ञानं ज्ञानिनस्तत्त्वदर्शिनः ॥

tad viddhi praṇipātēna pariprasnēna sēvayā
upadēkṣyanti tē jñānaṁ jñāninaḥ tattva-darśinaḥ

Baba: Please explain the meaning word by word.

Nana: '*tad viddhi praṇipātēna*' means a devotee should approach his Guru for knowledge by prostrating to him.

Baba: Mere prostrating is not enough, one has to have, **सर्वस्व शरणागति** (*sarvasva śaraṇāgati*), complete surrender to the *Sadguru.*

Nana: Paripraśna means ask questions.

Baba: Praśna is a question, *paripraśna* means one should not merely ask questions out of idle curiosity or with any improper motive to catch mistakes in the *Guru*'s answer, but with a serious genuineness and with a desire to achieve *moksha* or spiritual progress.

Nana: Sēvayā! Perform *sēva*, service to the *Guru.*

Baba: Sēva is not rendering service, by retaining the feeling that one is free to offer or refuse it. One must feel that he is not the master of his body, but his body belongs to the *Guru* and exists merely to render service unto Him.

Nana: Jñāninaḥ, the *Guru* who is a *jñāni*, '*tattva-darśinaḥ*' having attained realization of the Divine '*upadēkṣyanti tē jñānaṁ*' gives *upadēsha* or instruction, to the disciple of the knowledge of self-realization.

Baba: Can any other word be read instead of *jñānam*?
Nana: Yes *Baba*! It can also be read as

"*upadēkṣyanti tē ajñānaṁ*"

Baba: That is the true intent. Guru directs or indicates to the disciple as to what is *ajñānaṁ* so that the disciple can discard it and attain his/her true state, which is *jñāna swaroopa*.

The disciple is under the delusion, the root ignorance, that he/she is the body, he/she is a creature (*jīva*), that God (*Brahman*), and the world are different from him/her. This is an error inherited from innumerable past births. *Upadēsha* is merely to show this error and destroy the ignorance.

अथर्वाङ्गिरसः पुच्छं प्रतिष्ठा।
atharvāṅgīrasaḥ pucchaṁ pratiṣṭhā

Where does the mind-body get established in culmination?

It gets established in *Atharva* and *Aṅgīrasa*. The etymological meaning of both these words is given as fire. Philosophically, according to Chandogya Upaniṣad (CU-1.2.10) [3] *Aṅgīrasa* is "the rasa (essence) of the angas (limbs)". So *Aṅgīrasa* can be understood as the essence of various branches of knowledge.

How is the Essence Obtained?
Knowledge when practiced on a daily basis (निधिध्यासा *nidhidhyāsā*) transforms into **Skill**. The **Skill**, when per-

fected over time, results in a **Balanced mind**. From this **Balance**, arises the **Insight** (the essence), that **one is the *ātman* and not the body.** *Nidhidyasa*, the day-to-day practice of knowledge from the *Yajurvēda, Rigvēda*, and *Samavēda*, culminates in the aspects of both ***Aṅgīrasa*** and ***Atharva***.

Atharva also has reference to Fire or *Agni tattwam.* So, constantly remembering the *Guru's Ādēśa* burns away the past impressions and renders the *chitta* pure.

Just as the *prāṇa* body culminated in *Pṛthvī tattwa*, which has been understood as *steadiness of mind*, so also, the mind body culminates in *Aṅgīrasa* (*Āpah*) *tattwa*, which represents *the essence of various branches of knowledge* and *Atharva* or *Agni tattwam*, which represents the fire that burns away our past impressions.

तदप्येष श्लोको भवति॥

tadapyēṣa śhlokō bhavati [3.22]

The essence of knowledge and truth is described in a compact, poetic, and structured language.

At the end of manōmaya kōśa, the buddhi aspect of the mind is illumined with the above insight, and the chitta aspect is purified.

An Illumined Mind

A Physics Perspective:

States Of Equilibrium [20]:

A body is said to be in a state of equilibrium when the net forces acting on the body are zero. The nature of equilibrium is known from the motion that the body executes when it is subjected to a small disturbance. This analysis leads to three states of equilibrium: unstable, stable, and neutral equilibrium.

Unstable Equilibrium:

If the system moves away from the equilibrium due to small disturbances, then the equilibrium is said to be unstable. In an unstable equilibrium, the body tends to go on increasing its displacement from the equilibrium position. In this type of equilibrium, any departure of the system from equilibrium gives rise to forces or tendencies that move the system further away from equilibrium.

For example, consider a ball at rest on top of an inverted bowl. If it is given a slight push, it will roll down from the surface, and goes far away from its original equilibrium position.
This can be compared to people with an immature state of mind. When all desires are satisfied, they are apparently happy and seem to be enjoying an equilibrium state. But even a small variation from their expectation, for in-

stance, a setback in an examination or in love, and they tend towards depression or a state of despair. These are seekers who overtly profess their devotion when their desires are fulfilled and will run to another guru when their smallest desires do not materialize. This state can be compared to that of a closed mind akin to an inverted bowl.

Stable Equilibrium:

A body at rest is in stable equilibrium if, when slightly displaced, it returns to its original position. Any departure from the equilibrium state gives rise to forces or influences that return the system to its state of equilibrium. For example, a small push given to a ball in a bowl will cause it to oscillate back and forth about the equilibrium position and finally return to its original still state.

This is akin to a person with a mature mind who has had several setbacks and realizes that happiness is an interval between two sorrows. These are spiritual seekers whose faith may have oscillated earlier, but reach a state of equilibrium in due course. Such seekers have an open mind. But, they are also stuck in a well, constituting preconceived notions from their individual experiences, which precondition their mind while facing new circumstances. Hence, they tend to have a typical doubting mind that oscillates at every new circumstance.

Neutral or Steady-state Equilibrium:

For a body at rest in neutral equilibrium, a slight change will not necessarily lead to the system returning to the prior state, but it will not begin to diverge from its state of equilibrium, either.

For example, consider a ball on a flat table. Push it slightly, and it will roll a bit and settle on another spot on the table. The disturbance affected the position, but not the stability. This state of equilibrium possessed by a body will stay at rest despite being moved into a new position; it will neither move back to its original position nor move on any further.

This state is achieved when the walls of the metaphorical well are pushed and the well is expanded as a consequence of knowledge developed through learning from trials and tribulations. This can also be achieved with faith in one's *Guru* and His teachings. Finally, the seekers overcoming and learning from several hardships reach a state of Complete equilibrium, and perceive everything as the Lord's Will. Such a state of complete surrender can be called a balanced state of mind or an illumined mind, the true state of a *Jñāni*, a person of Wisdom.

Summary

यजुः ***Yajus*** *or Sacrifice (of untruth), is the highest form of thought, that takes one to the Truth.*

ऋक् ***ṛk***, *is to praise or to shine, in the form of metrical mantras, that takes one from the darkness of ignorance to the light of knowledge.*

साम ***Sāma***, *is to sing or to sooth, in a melodious manner, to bring peace or harmony, thereby taking one from a state of mortality to the highest state of immortality.*

*These branches of knowledge indicate (**ādēśa**) the ātman as the reality. Through practice of this knowledge, in day-to-day life, the culmination is **manōmaya body being consecrated** with **illumination of the mind**, the Buddhi Aspect, and also **purification of the mind**, the Chitta Aspect.*

Considering the mind as a mirror, one observes that illumination is a result of the essence of knowledge obtained through practice, a reflection of the "*āpah tattwam*" and the purity of *chitta* is obtained through the fire of detachment accrued due to sacrifice of untruth through '*neti, neti*' that is a reflection of "*agni tattwam*".

One is able to see the reflection of their 'Self' in the mirror of a steady, illumined, and pure mind and 'indicating' to it there 'I am'. But, this self is still limited by the sense of Ahaṃkāram, ahaṃ akāram, 'I am this physical form', the incorrect identification with the body.

Manōmaya Kōśa

यतो॒वा॒चो निवर्तन्ते। अप्रा॑प्य॒ मन॑सा स॒ह।
आनन्दं ब्रह्म॑णो वि॒द्वान्। न बिभेति कदा॑चने॒ति।

yatō vāchō nivar'tan'tē [4.1]
ap'rāāp'ya manasā saha [4.2]
ānan'daṁ' brah'maṇō vid'vā-ne [4.3]
na bibhēti kadāchanēti [4.4]

तस्यैष एव शारीर॑ आ॒त्मा। यः पूर्व॒स्य। तस्माद्वा एतस्मा॑न्मनो॒मयात्।
अन्योऽन्तर आत्मा विं॑ज्ञान॒मयः। तेनै॑ष पूर्णः। स वा, एष पुरुषविंध, ए॒व।
तस्य पुरु॑षवि॒धताम्। अन्वयं॑ पुरुष॒विधः।

tas'yaiṣa ēva śhārīra ātmā [4.5] ya[fp]' pūr'vas'ya [4.6]
tas'mād'vā, ētas'māān'manōmayā-te [4.7]
an'yō'ntara āt'mā vij'ñānamayaḥa [4.8]
tē.naiṣha pūrṇaḥa [4.9]
sa vā, ēṣha puruṣhavidha, ēva [4.10]
tas'ya puruṣhavidhatām [4.11]
anvayaṁ' puruṣhavidhaḥa [4.12]

तस्य श्रंद्धैव॒ शिरः। ऋतं दक्षिं॑णः प॒क्षः। सत्यमुत्त॑रः प॒क्षः। योग॑ आ॒त्मा।
महः पुच्छं॑ प्रति॒ष्ठा। तदप्येष श्लों॑को भ॒वति॥

tas'yash' śhraddhaiva śhiraḥ [4.13]
ṛtaṁ' dak'ṣhiṇa[fp]' pakṣhaḥa [4.14]
sat'yamut'tara[fp]' pakṣhaḥa [4.15] yōga, ātmā [4.16]
maha[fp]' puch'chhaṁ pratiṣh'ṭhā [4.17]
tadap'yēṣhash śhlōkō bhavati [4.18]

Limitations of Mind and Speech

The seeker can see the reflection of the Self in the pure, illumined, and steady mind. But, what is being witnessed, even though it is only a reflection, is beyond the reach of the mind and is hence incapable of expression in words. This experience is captured in the verses:

यतो वाचो निवर्तन्ते। ***yatō vāchō nivartantē*** **[4.1]**

यतो *yatō* - From which वाचो *vāchō* speech - निवर्तन्ते *nivartantē* - The root निवर्त *nivarta* - means "to return" or "to cease."

4.1 *Here, it refers to the fact that speech ceases to be effective in expressing the ultimate truth.*

अप्राप्य मनसा सह। ***aprāpya manasā saha*** **[4.2]**

अप्राप्य *aprāpya* - Not attainable or unattainable मनसा *manasā* - by the mind सह *saha* - together (with the speech).

4.2 *The knowledge of Brahman is unattainable by the mind.*

The ultimate reality, referred to as Brahman or ātman, cannot be attained through the limited capacity of the mind. The mind, with all its intellectual and perceptive faculties, is unable to reach or fully comprehend the absolute truth.

This verse points to the limitations of the mind in expressing the truth that is being seen as reflected in it, and emphasizes the need for higher spiritual practices, direct experience, or a form of realization that transcends mental effort.

आनन्दं ब्रह्मणो विद्वान्। न बिभेति कदाचनेति।
ānandaṁ brahmaṇō vidvān [4.3]
na bibhēti kadāchanēti [4.4]

आनन्दं *ānandaṃ* - *Ānanda* or Bliss ब्रह्मणो *brahmaṇō* - of Brahman विद्वान् *vidvān* - knower.

4.3 *The knower of Brahman knows Bliss.*

न - *na* Not बिभेति *bibhēti* - afraid कदाचनेति *kadāchanēti* - in any moment ever.

4.4 *He has no fear at any time ever.*

These two aspects of the experience of Bliss and the absence of Fear are key to distinguishing mere intellectual understanding from actual realisation of the Self. Hence, the mind sheath, even though it throws light on the truth through the intellectual discourse, it does not lead to grasping its direct experience.

It's like seeing a burning flame but unable to experience either its light or its warmth. Just as one sees and hears about the apple and gains all knowledge about it, but can not express its sweetness, as one has not eaten it, so also, inspite of gaining all knowledge about the *Brahman*, one is incapable of either expressing its true nature, which is Bliss, or enjoy a complete state of fearlessness, as one has not attained its direct experience.

Identification of an Inner Self

तस्यैष एव शारीर आत्मा। यः पूर्वस्य।

tasyaiṣa ēva śārīra ātmā **[4.5]** ***yaḥ pūrvasya*** **[4.6]**

तस्यैष *tasyaiṣa* - Of that (talking of which) this (mind-body) एव *ēva* - indeed शारीर आत्मा *śārīra ātmā* - is the embodied self, यः *yaḥ* - of one who पूर्वस्य *pūrvasya* - is related to the earlier one (the *prāṇa* body sustained by the vital breath).

4.5, 4.6 ***This mind body is indeed the embodied self of the one which is related to the earlier one, that is, the prāṇa body.***

Just as *prāṇa* is the subtlest of the food that sustains the body, the mind is the subtlest aspect that sustains the *prāṇa*. One can sustain the lifespan of one's body by the power of one's will.

In Rāmayana, Rishi Sarabhanga, through sheer will power, sustained his life by controlling his breath, to have the darshan of Lord Rāma.

तस्माद्वा एतस्मान्मनोमयात्।

tasmādvā ētasmānmanōmayāt **[4.7]**

तस्माद्वा *tasmāt* - From that point of view, verily एतस्मात् *ētasmāt* - hence this मनोमयात् *manōmayāt* - mind is filled with.

4.7 ***Similar to how the prāṇamaya body is filled with the manōmaya, verily, this mind body is***

filled with ...

अन्योऽन्तर आत्मा विज्ञानमयः।

anyō'ntara ātmā vijñānamayaḥ [4.8]

अन्यः *anyaḥ* - another अन्तर *antara* - inner आत्मा *ātmā* - self (after mind) is विज्ञानमयः *vijñānamayaḥ* - filled with that of wisdom.

4.8 *...another inner self, is that of wisdom*

This mind comprises an inner self, wisdom, which is the capability to Love all. It is the capability to see the **Oneness** within the vastly prevalent diversity.

तेनैष पूर्णः। *tēnaiṣa pūrṇaḥ* [4.9]

तेन *tēna* - By that (*vijñāna* or wisdom) एषः *ēṣaḥ* - this (mind) पूर्णः *pūrṇaḥ* - is filled of.

4.9 *The mind-body is filled with that of wisdom or vijñāna śarīra.*

Just as the entire physical form is filled with the vital energy or *prāṇa*, and the entire *prāṇa* form is filled with the mind, so also, the mind form is filled with *vijñāna* or wisdom.

स वा एष पुरुषविध एव।

sa vā ēṣa puruṣavidha ēva [4.10]

स *sa* - That (*vijñāna*) वा *vā* - verily has एष *ēṣa* - this पुरुषविध *puruṣavidha* - form of *puruṣa* एव *ēva* - itself.

4.10 *This vijñāna has verily a form similar to a human being itself.*

तस्य पुरुषविधताम्। ***tasya puruṣavidhatām*** [4.11]

तस्य *tasya* - That (*vijñāna*) पुरुषविधताम् *puruṣavidhatām* - has the form or nature of *puruṣa.*

4.11 ***That vijñāna śarīra has the form or nature of puruṣa***

अन्वयं पुरुषविधः। ***anvayaṁ puruṣavidhaḥ*** [4.12]

अन्वयं *anvayaṁ* - Here is the correspondence of *vijñāna* (similar to) पुरुषविधः *puruṣavidhaḥ* - the form of *puruṣa.*

4.12 ***Here is the correspondence of vijñāna similar to the form of puruṣa.***

Summary

There is another inner layer comprising wisdom with which the mind sheath is filled. Just as the entire physical form is filled with prāṇa, and the entire prāṇa form is filled with mind, so also, the entire mind sheath is filled with wisdom. This wisdom-body has, verily, a form similar to that of a human being itself, and its description is similar to that of puruṣa.

Description of *Vijñānamaya Śarīra*

तस्य श्रद्धैव शिरः। *tasya śraddhaiva śiraḥ* [4.13]

4.13 ***It has śraddha (Utmost Faith) as its Head***

ऋतं दक्षिणः पक्षः। *ṛtaṁ dakṣiṇaḥ pakṣaḥ* [4.14]

4.14 ***Ṛtam (Cosmic Order) as its right aspect.***

सत्यमुत्तरः पक्षः। *satyamuttaraḥ pakṣaḥ* [4.15]

4.15 ***Satyam (Existence) as its left aspect.***

योग आत्मा। *yōga ātmā* [4.16]

4.16 ***Yōga (Union with the Divine) as its Self or central aspect.***

महः पुच्छं प्रतिष्ठा। *mahaḥ pucchaṁ pratiṣṭhā* [4.17]

4.17 ***Mahat or Intelligence principle as its resting abode at the lower end.***

Here, faith is considered as the highest (*śiraḥ*) form of thought. The will power is guided by faith. ṛtaṃ is the working aspect of faith. When one has faith that one is *atman* and not the body, then one always acts (*dakṣiṇaḥ*) in accordance with their conscience, that is, in a righteous manner. Even higher (*uttara*) dimension is to live in accordance with Truth, *Satyam*, at all times. That is, to always be aware of the divinity within all beings. This leads one to unite (*yōga*, with root word *yuj*, meaning union) with the divine self. This understanding indeed culminates in the *mahat* or intelligence principle.

तदप्येष श्लोको भवति।
tadapyēṣa śhlōkō bhavati [4.18]

4.18 The essence of knowledge and truth is described in a compact, poetic, and structured form.

Philosophical Perspective of Vijñānamaya Śarīra:

- **तस्य श्रद्धैव शिरः।** ***tasya śraddhaiva śiraḥ***

It is said,
" श्रद्धावान् लभते ज्ञानम्।" "*śraddhāvān labhatē jñānam*".

He who has *complete faith in the scripture or in the words of their Guru*, the very embodiment of knowledge, will attain *jñānam* or wisdom. Hence, *śraddha* is indeed the head of the wisdom body or the highest state of the mind, where reason ceases to exist.

A Small Anecdote

Arjuna and Krishna were walking through the woods, on the eve of the war day, and the following conversation takes place:
Krishna: Arjuna! See how beautiful that peacock is!
Arjuna: Yes, Krishna! The peacock is indeed beautiful.
Krishna: No, Arjuna. See carefully, it is *Garuda*, the Eagle
Arjuna: Yes, Lord. It is indeed *Garuda.*
Krishna: No, No, Arjuna, it seems to me to be a Pigeon, a Dove!
Arjuna: Oh! Krishna! Yes, it is a Pigeon.
Krishna: What is this, Arjuna? Don't you have your

mind to correctly decipher as to what bird it is?
Arjuna: Oh! Lord! How do You expect me to believe my eyes? If I say it is a Peacock, you might change it to an Eagle. If I dare say it is an Eagle, you may change it to a Pigeon. I trust your word more than my eyes or my mind. This complete faith in the Lord is what resulted in Krishna blessing Arjuna with the *Bhagavad Gita*, the essence of all the *vēdas* and *Upanishads*, on the battlefield.

ऋतं दक्षिणः पक्षः। *Ṛtam dakṣiṇaḥ pakṣaḥ*

Ṛtam is the karma aspect of wisdom.
Ṛtam is the Cosmic Order that one witnesses in the Universe. For example, in physics, we have been able to discover the laws governing planetary motion, and those of objects on Earth are the same. This suggests, there is an intelligence that governs the whole Universe. Similarly, our actions must also align with that of the Universal order.
For example, we observe that all planets move in their respective orbits, interact with other objects in the universe, but do not disturb the orbits of others.

Similarly, we should conduct ourselves in such a way that we enjoy our lives through various interactions without disturbing the rights of other beings to enjoy their lives. **This is called Righteous Conduct or *Dharma*.** This is indeed the working aspect of *vijñāna*.

In Telugu, there is a beautiful saying

నొప్పింపక తా నొవ్వక తప్పించుకు తిరుగువాడె ధన్యుడు సుమతి
"noppimpaka tā novvaka tappiñchuku tiruguvāḍe dhanyuḍu sumati"

"Oh! Man with an equanimous mind! The one who can journey through life delightfully, by neither hurting others nor hurting oneself, is indeed a blessed one".

सत्यमुत्तरः पक्षः। *satyamuttaraḥ pakṣaḥ*

Satyam is *uttara pakṣaḥ* or higher aspect of wisdom.

In regard to *Satyam*, the following is said:

"सत्यं ब्रूयात्" ; आधिभौतिकम्
"satyaṁ brūyāt"; ādhibhautikam (Physical level)
"प्रियं ब्रूयात्" ; आधिदैविकम्
"priyaṁ brūyāt"; ādhidaivikam (Intellectual level)
"न ब्रूयात् सत्यम् अप्रियम्" ; आध्यात्मिकम्
"na brūyāt satyam apriyam"; ādhyātmikam (Spiritual level)

"One should always tell the Truth, but one should speak it in such a way that it is pleasant to the one who is being spoken to. It should not disturb the listener's mental demeanour; else, were one to consider that the truth one wishes to communicate is unpleasant, then one should completely refrain from speaking it."

योग आत्मा। *yōga ātmā*

For ***yōga***, the root word is ***yuj***, meaning **"Union"**. So, this connotes **"Union with the Divine (Self)"**.

This translates to Unity between **Thought** (*śraddha*), **Word** (*Satyam*) and **Deed** (*Ṛtam*).

That's why, it is said
मनस एकम् , वचस एकम् , कर्मण्येकम् महात्मनम्
manasyēkaṁ vacasyēkaṁ karmaṇyēkaṁ mahātmanām

The one who has unity (*ēkaṁ*) in thought (*manas*), word (*vachas*), and deed (*karmani*) is indeed a great person (*mahātma*). That is, *ātma* or self, which is immersed in *mahat tattwa.* Mahat means great. It is the essence of intelligence (*buddhi tattwa*), which is pure *chitta.* The one who follows this path gets established in *Mahat.*

Yōga **in** ***Jñāna*** **and** ***Karma***

In *Patanjali yōga sutras* (1.2) [21], it is said,
योगः चित्तवृत्तिनिरोधः *yōgaḥ chitta-vṛtti-nirodhaḥ*

Yōga is the cessation or restraint of all mental modifications. There are five types of vṛttis:
1. **प्रमाण** *pramāṇa*: Right knowledge
2. **विपर्यय** *viparyaya*: Wrong knowledge or Misperception
3. **विकल्प** *vikalpa*: Imagination without any basis of reality
4. **निद्रा** *nidrā*: Sleep or Mental Inertia
5. **स्मृति** *smṛti*: Memory or Past impressions

This yōga is achieved through meditation, the path of jñāna.

In the *Bhagavad Gita*, Sri Krishna says (2.50) [19]
योगः कर्मसु कौशलम् *yōgaḥ karmasu kauśalam*
Yōga is excellence in actions, especially one's duties.
Yōga is not merely a mechanical action, but acting with full awareness, detachment from outcome, and in harmony with *Dharma*.
Here, one achieves yōga through selfless action or the path of karma.

Personal Experience

In 2009, I had gone on a trip to *Kailash Manasarovar* along with my students and friends, but could not get a Chinese Visa. In Nepal, we had the *darshan* of Lord *Pashupatinath* and *Mansa Devi* and visited other places of worship, and came back late at night. Following my routine, I woke up at 5 am, offered my *suprabhatam* (morning prayer). And then, returned to sleep.
Swami appeared in my dream and asked me, "What do you want?"
I said, *Swami!* Please bless me with devotion to your Lotus feet.

Swami said, Take *padanamaskaram.* I fell at His Lotus feet, and when I got up, *Swami* said three words with a pregnant pause:

1. **एकाग्रता** *Ekāgratā*
2. **आत्मतत्त्वम्** *Ātma tattwam*
3. **ऐक्यता** *Eikyata*

Then, I got up and was very thrilled that *Swami* blessed me with His *Darśanam, Sparśanam*, and *Saṃbhāṣaṇam*. That is, *Swami* blessed me with vision of His divine form, touch of His divine lotus feet and conversation filled with His divine nectarine words.

I was still just enjoying the moment, and my friend sleeping next to me got up and asked me "Sastri Sir, you are glowing with Bliss! What happened?" On sharing my dream with him in detail, he asked, " What did you understand, sir?" I started thinking aloud and explained it as follows:

Ekāgratā* means, single pointed focus or concentration.** By ***ātma tattwam, I think, *Swami* is communicating that we should **contemplate that we are the *ātman*, and not the body**. Finally, ***Eikyata* means Unity**, that is, Swami is indicating that we should recognize, **the *ātman* within me is the same *ātman* in all beings**. I think *Swami* has given me a step-by-step process to move towards **"Constant Integrated Awareness"**.

My friend responded, "such a beautiful explanation, sir," and I replied, It is *Swami*'s grace that you woke and asked these questions with great enthusiasm so that I could grasp and consolidate this beautiful meaning from *Bhagavan*.

Swami blessed me with much more than what I could have earned completing the Kailash Mānasarovar yātra.

In *Bhāratīya* culture, we have a simple gesture to practice this important message.

Namaskāram

We greet each other with *Namaskāram* by folding both our palms together with the thumbs resting on ones heart. This word has three parts: *Na* + *maha* + *ākaram*. *Namaha* means "not me" and *ākaram* is the "physical form" consisting of 5 *karmēndriyas* (organs of action) and 5 *jñānēndriyas* (organs of perception), indicated by bringing together both palms (ten fingers). The act of placing them at the heart center indicates the presence of the Self at that point.
This is clearly explained in a verse in Nārayana Suktham [1], which goes thus:

पद्मकोशप्रतिकाशंगं् हृदयं चाप्यधोमुखम्।
अधो निष्ठ्य वितस्त्यन्ते नाभ्यामुपरि तिष्ठति॥

padma-kōśa-pratikāśagṁ hṛdayaṁ chāpy adhō-mukham
adhō niṣṭhya vitastyantē nābhyām upari tiṣṭhati

(The Self) appears like a (*padma-kōśa*) bunch of lotus petals, (*pratikāśagṁ*) all shining and (*adhō-mukham*) facing downwards, (*tiṣṭhati*) precisely located (*vitastyantē*) at the end of fully extended one-palm-span, from tip of little finger to tip of thumb, (*adhō*) downwards (*niṣṭhya*) from the Adam's apple and one-palm-span (*upari*) upwards (*nābhyām*) from the navel, called (*hṛdayaṁ*) the heart centre [22].

So, this gesture reminds us that we are **not the *dēha* but the *dēhi*** within. The person to whom the greeting is extended returns it in the same way, indicating they agree with this underlying truth.

महः पुच्छं प्रतिष्ठा। *mahaḥ puccharṁ pratiṣṭhā*

Mahat is considered the *buddhi tattwa*, the intelligence principle.

In the inward journey, the wisdom or intelligence principle is to realise the underlying unity prevalent in the apparent diversity. This realisation, in practice, is translated as

"Love All, Serve All"

Thus, it culminates in the feeling of "*I Shall Love All Mankind*" and expands to the concept of "**सर्वभूतहिते रतः** *sarvabhūtahitē rataḥ*" which is "*Taking delight in the good of all living creatures*". This can be thought of as **Expansion Love**.

Summary

यजुः *yajuḥ* - ***śraddha*** *or Utmost Faith, is the highest form of wisdom, that takes one to the path of Love.*

ऋतं ***ṛtaṁ***, *is Righteous Conduct.*

सत्यम ***satyam***, *is alignment with Highest Truth.*

योग आत्मा ***yōga ātmā*** *is Union with the Divine, achieved as Constant Integrated Awareness.*

महः पुच्छं प्रतिष्ठा ***mahaḥ puccharṁ pratiṣṭhā*** *This is established in Expansion Love, the true intelligence. Con-*

*sidering mind as mirror, one observes that this expansion Love is reflection of the expansive nature of Vāyu. Through practice of "**Love All Serve All**", in day-to-day life, the **Vijñānamaya** body is consecrated with **elimination of ego**, the Ahaṃkāra Aspect of the mind. One loses body consciousness and lives in ātmic consciousness.*

Vijñānamaya Kōśa

विज्ञानंयज्ञं तंनुते। कर्माणि तनुतेऽपिंच। विज्ञानं देवाः सर्वें।
ब्रह्मज्येष्ठमुपांसते। विज्ञानं ब्रह्म चेद्वेदं। तस्माच्चेन्न प्रमाद्यंति।
शरीरें पाप्मंनो हित्वा। सर्वान् कामान् समश्नुंत, इति।

vijñānam yajñam' tanutē [5.1]
kar'māṇi tanutē'pi cha [5.2]
vijñānam dēvā' sar'vēe [5.3]
brah'maj' jyēṣh'ṭhamupāsatē [5.4]
vijñānam brah'ma ched'vēda [5.5]
tas'māch'chēn'nap' pramādyati [5.6]
śharīrē pāpmanō hit'vā [5.7]
sar'vān' kāmān' samaśh'nuta, ¡iti [5.8]

तस्यैष, एव शारींर आत्मा। यःपूर्वस्य।
तस्माद्वा, एतस्माद्विंज्ञानमयात्।
अन्योऽन्तर, आत्मांऽऽनन्दमयः। तेनैंष पूर्णः।
स वा, एष पुरुषविंध, एव।
तस्य पुरुंषविधताम्। अन्वयं पुरुषविधः।

tas'yaiṣha, ēva śhārīra, ātmā [5.9]
ya[fp]' pūr'vas'ya [5.10]
tas'mād'vā, ētas'mād'vijñānamayā-te [5.11]
an'yō (a)n'tara, āt'mā (a)nan'damayaḥa [5.12]
tenaiṣha pūr'ṇaḥa [5.13]
sa vā, ēṣha puruṣhavidha, ēva [5.14]
tas'ya puruṣhavidhatām [5.15]
an'vayam' puruṣhavidhaḥa [5.16]

तस्य प्रियंमेव शिरः। मोदो दक्षिंणः पक्षः।
प्रमोद उत्तंरः पक्षः। आनंन्द आत्मा। ब्रह्म पुच्छं प्रतिष्ठा।

tasya priyameva śhiraḥ [5.17]
mōdō dakṣhiṇa[fp]' pakṣaḥ [5.18]
pramōda, ut'tara[fp]' pak'ṣhaḥa [5.19]
ānan'da, āt'mā [5.20]
brahma puch'chhaṁ' pratiṣh'ṭhā [5.21]

तदप्येष श्लोंको भवति।
tadap'yēṣhash' śhlōkō bhavati [5.22]

The Process of Yajña

विज्ञानं यज्ञं तनुते। *vijñānaṁ yajñaṁ tanutē* [5.1]

विज्ञानं *vijñāna* - is *Viśeṣa Jñāna*, discriminative knowledge or higher knowledge.
That which is obtained through careful introspection and refinement, is referred to as wisdom of spiritual nature.
यज्ञं *yajñaṃ* - sacrifice; तनुते *tanutē* - manifests, extends, initiates, performs;

5.1 *Vijñāna* (discriminative knowledge) extends or manifests the *yajña* (sacrifice).
Vijñāna, the discrimination knowledge between truth and untruth, initiates the process of sacrifice of untruth and acceptance of truth.

Yajña is generally perceived as the sacrificial fire in which समिध् *samidh* - (i.e., wooden sticks) burn as an oblation of Ghee is made.

How is Ghee obtained?

Milk is curdled by the fermentation process. Butter is obtained by churning the curd. It floats in the buttermilk. Finally, the process of heating the butter separates the Ghee from its impurities.

In a similar manner: *Vēdas are the milk (source of knowledge), which transform into curd (accumulation and internalization of ideas) through the process of* श्रवण *Śravaṇa (listening).*
The process of churning (reflection) is referred to as मनन *Manana, which brings forth the heart filled with compassion and kindness (butter) floating in the sea of* संसार *Saṃsāra, (buttermilk).*
Finally, by निदिध्यासन *Nididhyāsana or* तपस् *Tapas, i.e., through the fire of internal discipline (the process of heating the butter), one obtains the refined intellect (Ghee) that realizes: "I am* आत्मा *ātmā, not the body."*

With this refined intellect (Ghee), one sacrifices the feeling of body-consciousness (the समिध् *Samidh* or the wooden sticks), referred to as यज्ञः *Yajñaḥ* (sacrificial fire).

Thus, through this process of यज्ञः *Yajñaḥ (sacrifice of body consciousness), arises* विज्ञानम् *Vijñānam, Oneness (*आत्मिक-चेतना *Ātmika-chētanā) or Selfless Love. Yajña is an offering, a process of reflection, that leads to renunciation of untruth and acceptance of Truth.*

Through the process of yajña, a sacred offering or selfless action that prepares one to sacrifice their lower nature for embracing their higher nature, wisdom of spiritual nature is manifested or brought forth.

Spirituality is the process of transformation of a human being from animal nature to human nature to divine nature.

Love in Action

कर्माणि तनुतेऽपि च। ***karmāṇi tanutē'pi cha*** [5.2]

च *cha* - And, अपि *api* - additionally (this wisdom also) तनुते *tanutē* - brings forth कर्माणि *karmāṇi* - actions (filled with Love).
It has to be read with the previous line.

कर्माणि तनुतेऽपि च विज्ञानम्।
karmāṇi tanutē'pi cha vijñānam [5.2]

Wisdom also manifests or initiates actions, which in turn manifest vijñāna or wisdom.

Wisdom brings forth actions, inspired by Love and filled with Love.

Vijñāna body has faith as its head.

Where there is Faith,
There is Love.

Hence, Love is the underlying principle of wisdom. This wisdom, in the form of Love, permeates all the senses.

विज्ञानं देवाः सर्वे। ***Vijñānaṁ dēvā sarvē*** [5.3]

सर्वे *sarvē* - All देवाः *dēvā* - illumined beings विज्ञानं *vijñānaṃ* (are filled with this) Wisdom.

All Gods function through discriminative knowledge; All illumined beings are filled with this wisdom.

Alternatively, विज्ञानं *vijñānaṃ* - This wisdom देवाः सर्वे *dēvāḥ sarvē* - is expressed through all the senses in the form of Love.

5.3 *This wisdom is expressed through all the senses in the form of Love.*

Love in speech is Truth; Love in action is Dharma. The two wings of vijñānamaya body.

ब्रह्म ज्येष्ठमुपासते। ***brahma jyēṣṭhamupāsatē*** [5.4]

उपासते *upāsatē* - They worship ब्रह्म *Bramha* - the *Brahman* ज्येष्ठम् *jyēṣṭham* - who is the most venerable.

5.4 *They, the wise ones, worship the Brahman, who is the most venerable.*

ज्येष्ठ *jyēṣṭham* - These wise ones (those who are foremost of all beings) उपासते *upāsatē* - worship or meditate upon ब्रह्म *Brahman* - the Ultimate Reality.

These wise ones, who are the foremost of all human beings, worship or meditate upon the Brahman.

विज्ञानं ब्रह्म चेद्वेद। तस्माच्चेन्न प्रमाद्यति।

vijñānaṁ brahma chēdvēda **[5.5],**
tasmācchēnna pramādyati **[5.6]**

विज्ञान *vijñāna* - This wisdom चेद्वेद *chēdvēda* - bestows true knowledge of ब्रह्म *Brahman* - the Ultimate Reality.
तस्मात् *tasmāt* - Provided चेत् *chēt* - if न *na* - one is not प्रमाद्यति *pramādyati* - inattentive. That is, one should always be Watchful.

5.5, 5.6 ***This path of wisdom bestows true knowledge of Brahman, provided one is not inattentive.***

Summary

Vijñāna, the discrimination knowledge between Truth and untruth, initiates the process of sacrifice of untruth and acceptance of truth. Wisdom inspires actions filled with Love. This wisdom is expressed through all the senses in the form of Love.
Love in speech is Truth, and Love in action is Dharma.
Love in thoughts is Peace, and Love in feelings is Ahimsa.
Love is a heart filled with compassion.
These wise ones, the foremost of all beings, worship and meditate upon Brahman, the Ultimate Reality. This worship or meditation bestows true knowledge of Brahman, provided one is always watchful.

Watch Your
W- Words
A- Action
T- Thoughts
C- Character
H- Heart
WATCH
Fill them with
Sathya
(Truth)
Dharma
(Righteousness)
Shanti
(Peace)
Ahimsa
(Non-voilence)
Prema
(Love)
At All Times

Free from Sin

शरीरे पाप्मनो हित्वा। ***śarīre pāpmanō hitvā*** **[5.7]**

हित्वा *hitvā* - The act of renouncing शरीर *śarīra* - the body consciousness पाप्मनो *pāpmanō* - frees one from sin (the act of seeing duality instead of Unity).

5.7 The act of renouncing the body consciousness frees one from sin.

Vyāsa summarizes the entire 18 *puranas* into just two sentences [23]:

अष्टादश पुराणेषु व्यासस्य वचनद्वयम्।
परोपकारः पुण्याय पापाय परपीडनम्॥

aṣṭādaśa purāṇēṣu vyāsasya vacanadvayam
paropakāraḥ puṇyāya pāpāya parapīḍanam

To do service to others is a meritorious deed.
To cause harm to others is indeed a sin.

This has been further simplified by *Swami* as follows:

Help Ever. Hurt Never.

Later, *Swami* gave the inner spiritual meaning as
परोपकारः *paropakāraḥ* - (*Kara*) Those actions which take us (*upa*) - closer to (*Para*) - that Unity or Oneness (God) पुण्याय *puṇyāya* - are Meritorious.
पापाय *pāpāya* - Sin is परपीडनम् *parapīḍanam* - that which (*Pīḍanam*) - cuts asunder or divides (*Para*) - that Unity or Oneness (God).

Those actions which take us closer to that Unity or Oneness (God) are meritorius.
Those actions which divide that Unity or Oneness, that is, see duality (two) when there is only One, is Sin.

सर्वान् कामान् समश्नुत इति।
sarvān kāmān samaśnuta iti [5.8]

इति *iti* - Thus, सर्वान् *sarvān* - every कामान् *kāmān* - desire समश्नुत *samaśnuta* - is enjoyed or experienced सम *sama* - with equal mindedness (with no attachment whatsoever).

5.8 ***Thus, every desire is enjoyed or experienced with equal-mindedness (with no attachment whatsoever).***

Summary

The act of renouncing the body consciousness frees one from sin.
What is Sin?
Vyāsa summarizes the entire 18 *puranas* into just two sentences [23]:
To do service to others is a meritorious deed.
To cause harm to others is indeed a sin.
That is, **Help Ever. Hurt Never.**
A first step is to ensure one does not hurt others. This, in itself, would be a great help.
As a second step one must understand the dictum "परोपकारार्थम् इदं शरीरम्","paropakārārtham idaṁ śarīram".

That is, this body is given for the serive of others and plunge into selfless service to all.

In the third stage, one understands the inner meaning of "paropakāraḥ puṇyāya pāpāya parapīḍanam" as follows:

Those actions which take us closer to that Unity or Oneness (God) are meritorius.

Those actions which divide that Unity or Oneness, that is, see duality (two) when there is only One, is Sin.

Hence, one performs all actions with the awareness of the underlying unity, which is recognising the Lord's presence in everyone, and one becomes free from Sin.

Such a person reaches an exalted state of Oneness, wherein one enjoys everything with an equanimous mind with no attachment whatsoever.

Identification of Inner Self

तस्यैष एव शारीर आत्मा। यः पूर्वस्य।
tasyaiṣa ēva śārīra ātmā [5.9],
yaḥ pūrvasya [5.10]

तस्यैष *tasyaiṣa* - Of that (talking of which) This (*vijñāna*) एव *ēva* - indeed शारीर आत्मा *śārīra ātmā* - is the embodied self of यः *yaḥ* - the one who पूर्वस्य *pūrvasya* - is related to the earlier one (the mind body).

5.9, 5.10 The *vijñāna* body is indeed the embodied self of the one, which is related to the earlier one, that is, the mind body.

Vijñāna is the subtlest of the foods, that sustains the mind body. One can sustain the Will of one's mind by complete faith alone.

Rishi Sharabanga had complete faith that Lord Sri Rāma is an incarnation of Sri Mahā Vishnu and made up his mind (willed) to hold on to his breath till he was blessed with the darshan of the Lord, even though Indrā had come to take him to Brahma lōka, at his last moments on Earth.

तस्माद्वा एतस्माद्विज्ञानमयात्।
tasmādvā ētasmād vijñānamayāt [5.11]

तस्माद्वा *tasmādvā* - From that point of view, verily एतस्मात् *ētasmāt* - hence this विज्ञानमयात् *vijñānamayāt* - *vijñānamaya* body is filled with.

5.11 Similar to how the *manōmaya* body is filled

with *Vijñānamaya*, this wisdom sheath is filled with ...

अन्योऽन्तर आत्माऽऽनन्दमयः

anyō'ntara ātmānandamayaḥ [5.12]

अन्यः *anya* - Another अन्तर *antara* - inner आत्मा *ātmā* - self (after *vijñāna*) is आनन्दमयः *ānandamayaḥ* - filled with that of the *Ānanda*, absolute Bliss.

5.12 ...another inner self, is that of *Ānanda.*

This *vijñāna* comprises an inner self, *Ānanda*, which is the Bliss sheath.

तेनैष पूर्णः। ***tēnaiṣa pūrṇaḥ*** [5.13]

तेन *tēna* - By that (*Ānanda*) एषः *ēṣaḥ* - this (*vijñāna*) पूर्णः *pūrṇaḥ* - is filled of

5.13 *The vijñāna body is filled with that of Ānanda or Bliss*

Just as the entire physical form is filled with the vital energy or *prāṇa*, the entire *prāṇa* form is filled with the mind, and the mind form is, in turn, filled with *vijñāna* or wisdom, so also, the *vijñāna* form is filled with that of *Ānanda* or Bliss.

स वा एष पुरुषविध एव।

sa vā ēṣa puruṣavidha ēva [5.14]

स *sa* - That (*Ānanda* or Bliss) वा *vā* - verily has एष *ēṣa* - this पुरुषविध *puruṣavidha* - form of *puruṣa* एव *ēva* - itself.

5.14 *This Ānanda or Bliss has verily a form sim-*

ilar to human being itself and not different from it.

तस्य पुरुषविधताम्।

tasya puruṣavidhatām **[5.15]**

तस्य *tasya* - That (Ānanda) पुरुषविधताम् *puruṣavidhatām* - has the form or nature of *puruṣa.*

5.15 ***That Ānanda or Bliss has the form or nature of puruṣa.***

अन्वयं पुरुषविधः।

anvayaṁ puruṣavidhaḥ **[5.16]**

अन्वयं *anvayaṃ* - Here is the correspondence of *Ānanda* or Bliss (similar to) पुरुषविधः *puruṣavidhaḥ* - the form of *puruṣa.*

5.16 ***Here, is the correspondence of Ānanda similar to the form of puruṣa.***

Summary

There is another layer comprising Ānanda with which the wisdom sheath is filled. This Ānanda has, verily, a form similar to that of the human being itself, and its description is similar to that of puruṣa.

Description of *Ānandamaya Śarīra*

तस्य प्रियमेव शिरः। *tasya priyamēva śiraḥ* [5.17]

5.17 ***It has Enjoyment as its head.***

मोदो दक्षिणः पक्षः। *mōdō dakṣiṇaḥ pakṣaḥ* [5.18]

5.18 ***Delight as its right aspect.***

प्रमोद उत्तरः पक्षः। *pramōda uttaraḥ pakṣaḥ* [5.19]

5.19 ***Ecstacy as its left aspect.***

आनन्द आत्मा। *ānanda ātmā* [5.20]

5.20 ***Bliss as its Central or Core aspect.***

ब्रह्म पुच्छं प्रतिष्ठा। *brahma puccham̐ pratiṣṭhā* [5.21]

5.21 ***Brahman as its resting abode at the lower end.***

Philosophical Perspective of Ānandamaya Śarīra:

This resonates with the quote [24]:

Where there is Faith, there is Love;
Where there is Love, there is Peace;
Where there is Peace, there is Truth;
Where there is Truth, there is Bliss;
Where there is Bliss, there is God;
- Bhagavan Sri Sathya Sai Baba

The first line has already been discussed.
तस्य प्रियमेव शिरः। ***tasya priyamēva śiraḥ***
The highest form of wisdom is Love (*priyam*). For Love

is the underlying principle of the whole universe.

मोदो दक्षिणः पक्षः। ***mōdō dakṣiṇaḥ pakṣaḥ***

When we develop this Love, we enjoy Peace (*mōdam*).

How to develop this Love?

The easiest way to develop Love is to see the biggest blunders of others as insignificant and our smallest mistake to be unpardonable.

The external world is only a mirror of our internal world. So, all that we perceive in the world is but a reflection, reaction, and resound. Just as we touch up our face by looking in a mirror to remove any untidiness, so also, we need to purify our spiritual heart whenever we observe anything that is disturbing in the mirror, which is the world. This process is sometimes referred to, in the scriptures, as ज्ञातुम् (*jñātum*).

One says, "**I want Peace**". Observe that, when one removes this *ahaṃkāra*, 'I' and gives up 'want', the desire, then one attains Peace. *That is, when Love becomes part of our thoughts (filled with a feeling of unity) and actions (saturated with selflessness), we enjoy Peace.*

प्रमोद उत्तरः पक्षः। ***pramōda uttaraḥ pakṣaḥ***

When we thus Love ourselves reflected in the entire universe, we are living in the Truth, of Oneness of Creation, and we experience an expansive and transcendental form of Peace, *Pramōda.* This is referred to, in the scriptures, as द्रष्टुम् (*draṣṭum*).

आनन्द आत्मा। *ānanda ātmā*
When we loose ourselves in Love, we attain Bliss; Bliss is ātman (God). This is referred to, in the scriptures, as प्रवेष्टुम् (*pravēṣṭum*).

ब्रह्म पुच्छं प्रतिष्ठा। *brahma puccham pratiṣṭhā*
Finally, the entire dissolution of the individual culminates in the Ultimate Reality, *Brahman.*

Love is God. Live in Love

तदप्येष श्लोको भवति। *tadapyēṣa śhlōkō bhavati*
The essence of knowledge and truth is described in a compact, poetic, and structured language.

Summary

तस्य प्रियंमेवशिरः। *tasya priyamēva śiraḥ*
The highest form of vijñāna is Love (priyam).

मोदो दक्षिणः पक्षः। *mōdō dakṣiṇaḥ pakṣaḥ*
When we develop this Love, we enjoy Peace (mōdam).

प्रमोद उत्तरः पक्षः। *pramōda uttaraḥ pakṣaḥ*
The experience of an expansive and transcendental form of Peace is Pramōdam.

आनंन्द आत्मा। *ānanda ātmā*
Ātman or Self is Bliss.

ब्रह्म पुच्छंप्रतिष्ठा। *brahma puccham pratiṣṭhā*
At the very end, the individual self is established in the Universal Self, Brahman, the Ultimate Reality. The individual self is dissolved. Just as the river merges into

the ocean and has no identity left of its own, so too, the individual self ceases to exist and shines as the One Self.

The dissolution of the ego, is reflected in the '*mirror of the mind*' as the "*ākāśa tattwam*" which appears to be '*śūnyam*' (emptiness or void) but in reality is '*pūrṇam*' (fullness or completeness).

Ānandamaya Kōśa

असंन्नेव संभवति। अस॒द् ब्रह्मेति॒ वेद॒ चेत्।
अस्ति ब्रह्मेतिं चेद्वे॒द। सन्तमेनं ततो विंदुरि॒ति।
तस्यैष, एव शारीर, आ॒त्मा। यःपूर्व॒स्य।

asan'nēva sa bhavati [6.1]
asad'brah'mēti vēda chē-te [6.2]
as'tib' brah'mēti ched'vēda [6.3]
san'tamēnaṁ' tatō viduriti [6.4]
tas'yaiṣha, ēva śhārīra, ātmā [6.5]
ya[fp]' pūr'vas'ya [6.6]

अथातोंऽनुप्र॒श्नाः। उ॒ताविद्वा॒न॒मुं लो॒कं प्रेत्यं।
कश्च॒न गंच्छ॒ती३।
आहों वि॒द्वा॒न॒मुं लो॒कं प्रेत्य। कंश्चित्समंश्नु॒ता ३ उ॒।
सोंऽकामयत। ब॒हु स्यां॒ प्रजांये॒येतिं।

athātō nup'raśh'nā-ḥa [6.7]
utāvidvānamuṁ' lokaṁ' prēt'ya [6.8]
kaśh'chana gach'chhatī 3 [6.9]
āhō vid'vānamuṁ' lōkaṁ' prēt'ya [6.10]
kaśh'chit'samaśh'nutā 3 , u [6.11]
sō (a)kāmayata [6.12]
bahus' syāṁ' prajāyēyēti [6.13]

स तपोंऽतप्यत। स तपंस्तप्त्वा।
इदंगं सर्वंमसृजत। यदिदं किञ्चं।
तत् सृष्ट्वा। तदेवानुप्राविंशत्। तदंनुप्रविश्यं।

sa tapō'tap'yata [6.14] sa tapas'tap'tvā [6.15]
idagṁ' sar'vamasṛjata [6.16] yadidaṁ' kiñ'cha [6.17]
tat' sṛṣh'ṭvā [6.18]
tadēvānup'rāviśhate [6.19] tadanup'raviśh'ya [6.20]

सच्च त्यच्चांभवत्। निरुक्तं चानिंरुक्तं च।
निलयंनं चानिंलयनं च। विज्ञानं चाविंज्ञानं च।
सत्यं चानृतं च संत्यमभवत्। यदिंदं किंच।
तत्सत्यमिंत्याचक्षते। तदप्येष श्लोंको भवति॥

sach'chat' tyach'chābhavate [6.21]
niruk'taṁ' chāniruk'taṁ' cha [6.22]
nilayanaṁ' chānilayanaṁ' cha [6.23]
vijñānaṁ' chāvijñānaṁ' cha [6.24]
sat'yaṁ' chānṛtaṁ' cha sat'yamabhavate [6.25]
yadidaṁ' kiṁ cha [6.26]
tat'sat'yamit'yāchakṣhatē [6.27]
tadap'yēṣhash' śhlōkō bhavati [6.28]

Jñātum

Knowing the *Brahman* as Being

असन्नेव स भवति। *asannēva sa bhavati* [6.1]

असन *asan* - To be or To exist; असन्नेव *asannēva* - as if non-existent."; स *sa* - refers to *Brahmavid*; भवति *bhavati* - becomes.

6.1 *"Brahmavid, the Knower of Brahman, becomes as if non-existent."*

The individual having transcended the Ego (*ahaṃkāram: ahaṃ akāram*, the wrong identification of body as oneself) attains *Mōksha* (*mōha kshaya*, destruction of all attachment).

असद् ब्रह्मेति वेद चेत्। अस्ति ब्रह्मेति चेद्वेद।
asad brahmēti vēda chēt [6.2],
asti brahmēti chēdvēda [6.3]

चेत् *chēt* - If or "Does it happen that" वेद *vēda* - (*Brahmavid*) knows ब्रह्म *Brahma* - *Brahman* असद् *asad* - as non-existent इति *iti* - thus?

6.2 *Does one know (mistakenly) Brahman as non-existent?*

चेद्वेद *chēdvēda* - Does it happen that (*Brahmavid*) knows अस्ति ब्रह्म इति *asti brahma iti* - *Brahman* exists, thus?

6.3 *Does one know Brahman as existing (as being real)?*

सन्तमेनं ततो विदुरिति। ***santamēnaṁ tatō viduriti*** [6.4]

सन्तम् *santam* - existing, real; एनम् *ēnam* - this (Brahman); ततः *tataḥ* - therefore; विदुः *viduḥ* - they know; इति *iti* - thus;

6.4 *They know this (Brahman) as existing, as Sat (being).*

Or more emphatically,

6.4 *"Therefore, they know this (Brahman) as being."*

तस्यैष एव शारीर आत्मा। यः पूर्वस्य।
tasyaiṣa ēva śārīra ātmā [6.5],
yaḥ pūrvasya [6.6]

एषः *ēṣaḥ* - This शारीर आत्मा *śārīra ātmā* - embodied self एव *ēva* - is indeed तस्य *tasya* - That (*Brahman*) यः *yaḥ* - who was पूर्वस्य *pūrvasya* - previously mentioned.

6.5, 6.6 *"This (jīvātman), the embodied self, is truly the same as that earlier (paramātman), the Universal Self, that was described. He is not different; he is the very same in essence."*

Summary

Brahmavid, the Knower of Brahman, becomes as if non-existent. The individual having transcended the Ego (ahaṃkāram: ahaṃ akāram, the wrong identification of body as oneself) attains Mōksha (mōha kshaya, destruction of all attachment).

Then, there are two situations that arise.

Does one know (mistakenly) Brahman as non-existent?
Or
Does one know Brahman as existing (as being real)?
It is declared that,
They know this (Brahman) as existing, as Sat (Being).
Or more emphatically,
Therefore, they know this (Brahman) as being.
This (jīvātman), the embodied self, is truly the same as that earlier (paramātman), the Universal Self, that was described. He is not different; he is the very same in essence.

Draṣṭum

Perceiving The World of *Brahman*

अथातोऽनुप्रश्नाः। *athātō'nupraśnāḥ* [6.7]

अथ *atha*- Having completed listening to the *Shruti*, अतो *atō* - let us now therefore अनुप्रश्नाः *anupraśnāḥ* - look at the subsequent questions that follow, for deeper inquiry.

6.7 *Having completed listening to the Shruti (Sravana), let us now therefore, look at the subsequent questions that follow, for deeper enquiry.*

उताविद्वानमुं लोकं प्रेत्य। कश्चन गच्छती३।
utāvidvānamuṁ lōkaṁ prētya [6.8]
kaśchana gacchatī3 [6.9]

उत *uta* - Does अविद्वान् *avidvān* - an ignorant person प्रेत्य *prētya* - after passing away, referring to the transition after Death

Alternatively, प्रेत्य *prētya*: प्रति prati - towards + अय aya - going;

प्रेत्य *prētya* - *The transition from one state or realm to another*

In this context, it can be interpreted as transitioning from a state of mortality to a state of immortality.

अमुंलोकं *amuṃlōkaṃ* - (reach) that world or state (of *Brahman*)?

This is referred to as the immortal realm, attaining which there is no rebirth.

That is, after coming to comprehension (*Jñātum*) of the *Brahman*, one has to constantly live in the awareness (*Draṣṭum*) of the *Brahman*.

Summary

ho attains the state of immortality?

nly the knower (Jñātum) of Brahman.

ch a person enjoys a blissful state of Oneness, where erything is enjoyed in a detached manner.

w, the *Brahmavid* is able to witness (*Draṣṭum*) the steries of Creation as Divine Leela.

hman (and Brahmavid) desired, "May I become Many iving birth to Offspring, beings created in my own e."

man (and Brahmavid), having completed the auster- as again performed austerity, and Brahman (and navid) created all of this, whatever exists.

eeker, after attaining the world or state of *Brahman*, es *Brahmavid*, and desires to share their path to any more to tread on it and reach the same.

avid, along with *Brahman*, has once again under- he process of penance, the effort required to cre- Universe, after having already undertaken such s before. Here, the cyclical nature of Creation is zed.

ively, the *Brahmavid* has performed austerities to e Truth of Oneness and then He again embarked

So, the question raised here is:

6.8 ***Does an ignorant person transition from the cycle of birth and rebirth to that state of immortality?***

कश्चन *kaśchana* - Anyone (any such individual without the knowledge of *Brahman*) गच्छती *gacchatī* - ever attains that state of immortality?

6.9 ***Does any individual without having the knowledge of Brahman ever attain the state of immortality?***
No.

आहो विद्वानमुं लोकं प्रेत्य। कश्चित्समश्नुता ३ उ।
āhō vidvānamuṁ lōkaṁ prētya [6.10]
kaśchitsamaśnutā 3 u [6.11]

आहो *āho* - Or is it the case that विद्वान् *vidvān* - the knower of *Brahman* प्रेत्य *prētya* - transcends to अमुं *amuṃ* - that लोकं *lōkaṃ* - state of immortality?

6.10 ***Or, is it, the case that, the knower of Brahman transcends to that state of immortality?***
उ u This is for Sure.
In fact,
कश्चित् *kaśchit* - Someone who (knows the *Brahman*)
समश्नुता *samaśnutā* - experiences or enjoys a blissful state of Oneness, where everything is enjoyed in a detached manner.

6.11 ***Someone who knows the Brahman experi-***

ences or enjoys a blissful state of Oneness, where everything is enjoyed in a detached manner.
From here on, *Brahmavid*, who has dissolved into *Brahman*, can unravel the mysteries of Creation as Divine *Leela* (Sport).

सोऽकामयत। ***sō'kāmayata*** [6.12]

स: *saha* - *Brahman* and *Brahmavid* together have कामयत *kāmayata* - Desired (or Wished)

6.12 *Brahman and Brahmavid together desired*

बहुस्यां प्रजायेयेति। ***bahusyāṁ prajāyēyēti*** [6.13]

बहुस्यां *bahusyāṃ* - May I become Many प्रजायेयेति *prajāyēyēti* - by having offspring (referred to as beings created in my own image)

6.13 *"I wish that may I give birth to many".*

He (*Brahman* or *Brahmavid*) desired: 'Let me become many; let me be born (as many beings).

The seeker, after attaining the world or state of *Brahman*, becomes *Brahmavid*, and desires to share their path to help many more to tread on it and reach the same. For example, many realised masters, such as Mahātma Gautama Buddha, Sri Ādi Śaṅkarācārya, Sri Rāmakrishna Paramahamsa, Sri Paramahamsa Yōgānanda, Sri Ramana Maharishi, etc., have taken up the task of sharing their process of realisation with fellow seekers.

स तपोऽतप्यत। स तपस्तप्त्वा।
sa tapō'tapyata [6.14], ***sa tapastaptvā*** [6

स तपो *sa tapō* - One who performs austerity अ
ata - emphasizes the action (of performing
the past. तप्त्वा *taptvā* - indicates the comp
austerity) as a necessary step before anoth

6.14 The phrase "स तपोऽतप्यत *sa tapō'tapy*
to ***"He performed austerity"***, and

6.15 "स तपस्तप्त्वा *sa tapastaptvā*" transl
performed austerity" or ***"He, having austerity."***

Here, the cyclical nature of Creati
Brahmavid, along with *Brahman*, h
dertaken the process of penance, th
create the Universe, after having
such a process before.

Alternatively, the *Brahmavid* has p
realise the Truth of Oneness and t
on another journey of effort to b
Truth.

Just as Ganga (*Brahmavid*) un
tribulations (*tapas*) to reach t
then again has to further its e
also the *Brahmavid* after atta
through *tapas*, has to once ag
nearness to *Brahman*.

on another journey of effort to bring many more to this Truth.

Just as Ganga (*Brahmavid*) undergoes lots of trials and tribulations (*tapas*) to reach the Ocean (*Brahman*) and then again has to further its efforts (*tapas*) to enter it, so also the *Brahmavid* after attaining the world of *Brahman* through *tapas*, has to once again perform *tapas*, to attain nearness to *Brahman*.

Brahmavid perceives (*Draṣṭum*) that *Brahman* is immanent in the world as it's indwelling consciousness.

That is, "***Brahmavid*, after coming to comprehension (*Jñātum*) of the *Brahman*, constantly lives in the awareness (*Draṣṭum*) of the *Brahman*.**"

Pravēṣṭum

Entering the World of *Brahman*

इदंगं् सर्वमसृजत। यदिदं किञ्च।

idagṁ sarvamasṛjata **[6.16]**

yadidaṁ kiñcha **[6.17]**

These two phrases express the Creation or origin of everything. इदंगं् *idagṁ* - This or this very thing, सर्वम् *sarvam* - all or everything असृजत *asṛjata* - He created

6.16 "*He created all of this" or "He created everything".*

यत् *yat* - whatever; इदं *idaṃ* - this or this very thing; किञ्च *kiñcha* - anything.

6.17 '*Whatever this is' or 'Whatever exists'.*

He (the One) created all this - whatever this is.

The realised masters' set forth to create disciples who will create an organisation on the lines of the path laid down to them.

तत् सृष्ट्वा। तदेवानुप्राविशत्।

tat sṛṣṭvā **[6.18],** ***tadēvānuprāviśat*** **[6.19]**

The verb सृष्ट्वा *sṛṣṭvā* - (having created) shows that the Creation was completed before the action of entering.

अनुप्राविशत् *anuprāviśat* - Indicates that the creator entered into it.

"Entered into it", doesn't mean spatial entry, like entering a house, but existential immanence; it is the in-dwelling Consciousness (*antar-yāmin*).

6.18, 6.19 *"Having created that, He then entered it".*

Having created the Universe, the Creator entered it. Thus, every object, every being, is permeated by the divine.

'He created' could be understood as 'He willed' out of a creative impulse, due to the overflowing *ānanda* or Bliss.

Then, it becomes clear that, the very act of willing, is enough for the Creation to happen, and the Creation is but a natural, spontaneous flow of *ānanda*, the very nature of *Brahman*, just as waves are a spontaneous flow of water in the Ocean.
Having entered the Ocean, *Ganga* looses its identity completely and its essence is that of Ocean itself.

Alternatively, *Brahmavid* having created all this organised effort, has entered it in spirit.

तदनुप्रविश्य *tadanupraviśya* - "(*Brahman*) Having entered into that (Creation)",
अभवत् *abhavat* - became

- सत् च *sat cha* - "Being" or "the manifest" and असत् च *asat cha* - "Non-being" or "the unmanifest". "That which is" and "That which is not"
- निरुक्तं *niruktaṃ* - "That which can be explained" or defined by words and अनिरुक्तं *aniruktaṃ* - "That

which is beyond words".

- निलयनं *nilayanaṃ* - "That which is resting or settled (has a locus)" and अनिलयनं *anilayanaṃ* - "That which is non-resting or unsettled".

- विज्ञानं *vijñānaṃ* - Knowledge and अविज्ञानं *avijñānaṃ* - Ignorance.

  That is, *Brahman* is both the Known and the Unknown.

- सत्यं च *satyaṃ cha* - "That which is Truth (Reality)" and

  अनृतं च *anṛtaṃ cha* - "That which is Untruth (Illusion)."

सत्यमभवत् *satyamabhavat* - It (ultimately) became the Truth, the Ultimate Reality, despite manifesting many dualities.
यदिदं किञ्च - Whatever here, exists.
इति आचक्षते *iti āchakṣatē* - Thus, they declare तत् *tat* - That realisation of Ultimate Reality (alone) सत्यं *satyaṃ* - is the Truth.

Thus, they declare, '*That realisation of Ultimate Reality*', is the Truth.

Summary

Brahmavid becomes as if non-existent, after the dissolution of Ego. Does he know Brahman to be existent or non-existent?
The knowers of Brahman, know this Brahman, as Sat

(Real) or Being.

The embodied Self is indeed the Universal Self. Both are same in essence.

Who attains the state of immortality?

Only the knower (Jñātum) of Brahman.

Such a person enjoys a blissful state of Oneness, where everything is enjoyed in a detached manner.

Now, the *Brahmavid* is able to witness (*Draṣṭum*) the mysteries of Creation as Divine Leela.

Brahman (and Brahmavid) desired, "May I become Many by giving birth to Offspring, beings created in my own image."

Brahman (and Brahmavid), having completed the austerity has again performed austerity, and Brahman (and Brahmavid) created all of this, whatever exists.

Having created it, Brahman (and Brahmavid) entered it.

Brahmavid perceives (*Draṣṭum*) that *Brahman* is immanent in the world as it's indwelling consciousness.

That is, ***Brahmavid*, after coming to comprehension (*Jñātum*) of the *Brahman*, constantly lives in the awareness (*Draṣṭum*) of the *Brahman* and finally enters (*Praveṣṭum*) into the very world of *Brahman*.**

That is, the *Brahmavid*'s entire world is saturated with that of *Brahman*.

Brahman (and Brahmavid) having entered the Creation, became all the apparent dualities, manifest/unmanifest, Truth/untruth, knowledge/ignorance, etc. Ultimately, all (whatever exists here) resolves into Satyam, the Real, the Eternal, and the Infinite. Thus, the wise ones declare, that this realisation of Ultimate Reality alone, to be the Truth.

Abhaya Prāpti

असुद्वा इदमग्रं, आसीत्। ततो वै सदंजायत।
तदात्मानं स्वयंमकुरुत। तस्मात् तत्सुकृतमुच्यंत इति।
यद्वैं तत्सुकृतम्। रंसो वैसः। रसग् ह्येवायं लब्ध्वानंन्दी भुवति।

asad' vā, idamag'ra, āsī-te [7.1]
tatō vai sadajāyata [7.2]
tadāt'mānag'gēs' svayamakuruta [7.3]
tas'māt' tat'sukṛtamuch'yata, iti [7.4]
yad'vai tat' sukṛtam [7.5] rasō vai saḥa [7.6],
rasag'gēh hyēvāyaṁ abdhvānandī bhavati [7.7]

को ह्येवान्याँत् कः प्राण्यात्। यदेष, आकाश, आनंन्दो न स्यात्।
एष ह्येवाऽऽनंन्द यांति।

kōh' hyēvān'yaāt' ka[fp]' prāṇ'yā-tē [7.8]
yadēṣa, ākāśha, ānan'dō nas' syā-tē [7.9]
ēṣhah' hyēvānan'da yāti [7.10]

युदा ह्येवैषुएतस्मिन्नदृश्येऽनात्म्येऽनिरुक्तेऽनिलयनेऽभयं प्रतिंष्ठां विन्दते।
अथ सोऽभयं गंतो भुवति।

yadāh' hyēvaiṣha ētas'min'nadṛśhyē
(a)nātmyē' (a)niruktē' (a)nilayanē'
(a)bhayaṁ pratiṣhṭhāṁ vindatē [7.11]
atha sō'bhayaṁ' gatō bhavati [7.12]

यदा ह्येवैष, एतस्मिन्नुदरमन्तरं कुरुते। अथ तस्य भयं भवति।
तत्वेव भयं विदुषोऽ मन्वानस्य। तदप्येष श्लोको भवति॥

yadāh hyēvaiṣha,
ētas'min'nudaraman'taraṁ' kurutē [7.13]
atha tas'ya bhayaṁ' bhavati [7.14]
tat'tvēva bhayaṁ viduṣhō man'vānasya [7.15]
tadap'yēṣhash' śhlōkō bhavati [7.16]

Brahmavid Brahmaiva Bhavati

असद् वा इदमग्र आसीत्। ततो वै सदजायत।
***asad vā idamagra āsīt* [7.1],**
***tatō vai sadajāyata* [7.2]**

अग्र *agra* - In the beginning, वा *vā* - indeed, इदम् *idam* - This (Universe) आसीत् *āsīt* - existed (or was) असद् *asat* - as non-being (or non-existent).
ततः *tatah* - From that, वै *vai* - Verily, सद् *sat* - Existence (Universe in manifest form) अजायत *ajāyata* - was born or came into being.

7.1, 7.2 *In the beginning, indeed, this (Universe) was non-existent or existed as Non-being. This non-being (or formless void) existed as the primordial state, and from it, the existence of the Universe (manifest form) came into being.*

In the beginning, indeed this (*Brahmavid*) existed as non-existent, when the individual self had been dissolved. And, from that, verily, the One Self emerged.

तदात्मानं स्वयमकुरुत।

tadātmānaṁ svayamakuruta [7.3]

तत् *tat* - That (*Brahman* or *Brahmavid*) आत्मानम् *ātmānam* - The Self (object form-"itself") स्वयम् *svayam* - By itself, of its own accord अकुरुत *akuruta* - Created, fashioned, made.

7.3 "*That Supreme Reality, by Itself, revealed Its own Self.*"

Or

7.3 *"Brahman (Brahmavid) manifests itself as the Self (ātman)-spontaneously and from within, indicating Self-reflective Consciousness"*.

तस्मात् तत्सुकृतमुच्यत इति।

tasmāt tatsukṛtamuchyata iti [7.4]

तस्मात् *tasmāt* - Therefore, तत् *tat* - That (manifestation of *Brahman* itself as the Self) इति *iti* - is thus उच्यते *uchyatē* - said to be सुकृतम् *sukṛtam* - a good deed or well made.

7.4 *Here, Brahman (Brahmavid) is praised as Sukṛta (well-made), not as something created by another, but because it is the intelligent, perfect source of Creation.*

यद्वै तत्सुकृतम्। ***yadvai tatsukṛtam*** [7.5]

यद् *yad* - That which वै *vai* - is indeed सुकृतम् *sukṛtam* - well-made is तत् *tat* - That (*Brahman*, the Ultimate Reality)

7.5 That which is indeed well-made, is That (Brahman or Brahmavid)

Or in a poetic sense:

7.5 "That alone is the perfectly fashioned and the very essence of all."

रसो वै सः। रसग् ह्येवायं लब्ध्वानन्दी भवति।

rasō vai saḥ [7.6]

rasa hyēvāyaṃ labdhvānandī bhavati [7.7]

वै *vai* - Indeed, सः *saḥ* - *Brahman* or *Brahmavid* is रसः *rasaḥ* - the ultimate essence or experience of delight within.

7.6 Indeed, Brahman (or Brahmavid) is the ultimate essence of experience of delight within.

रस *rasa* - Essence or The inner delight हि *hi* - indeed or verily एव *ēva* - is the only thing आयं *āyaṃ* - this one (the discerning seeker or *vivekin*) लब्ध्वा *labdhvā* - having obtained भवति *bhavati* - becomes आनन्दी *ānandī* - blissful.

7.7 "Verily, having attained (realized) that essence (rasa), this being becomes blissful."

Or, in a poetic sense:

7.7 "Having realized that Supreme Essence, Brahmavid becomes immersed in Bliss."

को ह्येवान्यात् कः प्राण्यात्।

ko hyēvānyāt kaḥ prāṇyāt [7.8]

को *ko* - Who? हि *hi* - indeed एव *ēva*- certainly / only अन्यात् *anyāt* - other than (*Brahman*) कः *kaḥ* - Who? प्राण्यात्

prāṇyāt would breathe / can breathe.

7.8a को ह्येवान्यात् *ko hyēvānyāt* - ***"Who indeed could breathe (live) if (the Self were) other (than One-self)?"***

7.8b कः प्राण्यात् *kaḥ prāṇyāt* - ***"Who could even breathe or live (if not for that Self)?"***

This is a contemplative rhetorical question that declares:

- The primacy of the Self (*Ātman*): It is the source of all life.
- Without the presence of *Brahman* or *Ātman*, no being could breathe or live.
- It refutes duality: there is no "other" by which we live.

  We live by That (*Brahman*) alone.

यदेष आकाश आनन्दो न स्यात्। एष ह्येवानन्द याति।

yadēṣa ākāśa ānandō na syāt [7.9],
ēṣa hyēvānanda yāti [7.10]

यदेष *yadēṣa* - If this आकाश *ākāśa* - Space or the first one emerging from Brahman;

Here, one could conceive this as chidākāśa, the same *nihitham guhayām*, the inherent cave of *buddhi*.

आनन्दः ānandaḥ - "Blissful" (*Brahman*'s nature) न स्यात् *na syāt* - were not, had it not been एषः *ēṣa* - This (individual or *jiva*) हि एव *hi ēva* - indeed verily याति *yāti* - attains आनन्द *ānanda* - Bliss.

7.9, 7.10 ***"If this ākāśa (which emerges from Brahman) were not itself Blissful, then this (jīva or Self) would not attain Bliss."*** This is what can be experienced by *Brahmavid*: '**The supreme effulgence**' which is the expression of *Brahman*.

यदा ह्येवैष एतस्मिन्नदृश्येऽनात्म्येऽनिरुक्तेऽनिलयनेऽभयं प्रतिष्ठां विन्दते।

yadā hyēvaiṣa ētasminnadṛśyē'nātmyē'niruktē' nilayanē' abhayaṁ pratiṣṭhāṁ vindatē [**7.11**]

यदा *yadā* - When हि एव *hi ēva* - indeed, truly एष *ēṣa* - this seeker or *jiva* प्रतिष्ठा *pratiṣṭhā* - gets established एतस्मिन *ētasmin* - in this Brahman अदृश्य *adṛśya* - that is invisible or unseen अनात्म्य *anātmya* - devoid of Ego or selfhood अनिरुक्त *anirukta* - indescribable अनिलय *anilaya* - without any support or base विन्दते *vindatē* - and attains अभयम् *abhayam* - fearlessness.

7.11 ***When the seeker truly realizes and becomes established in That (Brahman), that is invisible, devoid of ego, indescribable, and without any foundation, Brahmavid attains the supreme fearlessness.***

अथ सोऽभयं गतो भवति।

atha sō'(a)bhayaṁ gatō bhavati [**7.12**]

अथ *atha* - Then, thereafter सः *saḥ* -*Brahmavid* (the one who realises the Self) भवति *bhavati* - becomes one गतो *gatō* - who has attained अभयं *abhayaṃ* - fearlessness or freedom from fear.

7.12 "*Then the Brahmavid becomes one who has attained the fearless state.*"

"The *Brahmavid* abides in the Infinite *Brahman*, where there is no second, no fear."

यदा ह्येवैष एतस्मिन्नुदरमन्तरं कुरुते। थ तस्य भयं भवति।

yadā hyēvaiṣa ētasminnudaramantaraṁ kurute [**7.13**], ***tha tasya bhayaṁ bhavati*** [**7.14**]

यदा *yadā* - When हि एव *hi ēva*- indeed, truly एष *ēṣa* - this (individual or *jiva*) कुरुते *kurutē* - makes or creates अन्तरम् *antaram* - a distinction or difference उदरम् *udaram* - a gap or division or separation (even though literally it means stomach) एतस्मिन *ētasmin* - within this *Brahman.*

उदरम् अन्तरम् *udaram antaram* - is metaphorically 'a notion of separateness'. थ *tha* - Then, afterwards तस्य *tasya* - for the individual भयं *bhayaṃ* - fear भवति *bhavati* - arises.

7.13, 7.14 "*But when even the slightest gap or distinction is made in this (Brahman), then fear arises for him.*"

When one perceives duality - 'Self' versus 'other', or 'inner' versus 'outer' - then fear arises. The root of all fear is the notion of separation. **Only a person steeped in non-dual *Brahman* remains fearless.**

तत्वेव भयं विदुषो मन्वानस्य।

tatveva bhayaṁ viduṣo manvānasya [**7.15**]

तत् एव *tat ēva*- That alone भयं *bhayaṃ* - is the fear

विदुषः *viduṣaḥ* - of the one who knows partially, मन्वानस्य *manvānasya* - the one who reflects or contemplates but not fully realizes.

7.15 *Those who only intellectually reflect remain vulnerable to doubt and fear.*

तदप्येष श्लोको भवति॥ *tadapyēṣa śhlōkō bhavati*

The essence of knowledge and Truth through compact, poetic, and structured language.

Summary

In the beginning, indeed this (*Brahmavid*) existed as non-existent, when the individual self had been dissolved. And, from that, verily, the One Self emerged. That is, *Brahmavid* or *Brahman*, manifests itself as the Self (*ātman*) spontaneously and from within, indicating Self-reflective Consciousness and is praised as *Sukṛta* (well-made), not as something created by another, but because it is the intelligent, perfect source of Creation. That alone is the perfectly fashioned and the very essence of all. Indeed, *Brahman* (or *Brahmavid*) is the ultimate essence of experience of delight within.

Having realized that Supreme Essence, *Brahmavid* becomes immersed in Bliss, which is nothing but the Bliss of the supreme effulgence of *ākāśa*. When the seeker, thus, truly realizes and becomes established in That (*Brahman*), that is invisible, devoid of ego, indescribable, and without any foundation, *Brahmavid* attains the supreme fearlessness. For the *Brahmavid* abides in the Infinite *Brahman*, where there is no second, no fear.

"But when even the slightest gap or distinction is made in this (Brahman), then fear arises for him."

When one perceives duality - 'Self' versus 'other', or 'inner' versus 'outer' - then fear arises. The root of all fear is the notion of separation. **Only a person steeped in non-dual *Brahman* remains fearless.** Those who only intellectually reflect remain vulnerable to doubt and fear.

3

Levels of Ānanda

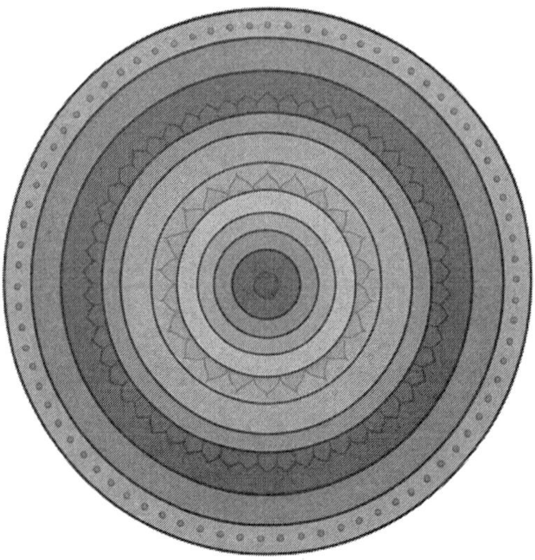

Grace of *Brahman*

भीषाऽस्माद्वातःपवते। भीषोदेति सूर्यः।
भीषाऽस्मादग्निंश्चेन्द्रश्च। मृत्युर्धावति पञ्चंम, इति।

bhīṣhā'smādvāta[fp]' pavatē [8.1]
bhīṣhōdēti sūr'yaḥa [8.2]
bhīṣā'smādag'niśh'chēn'draśh'cha [8.3]
mṛt'yur'dhāvati pañchama, iti [8.4]

भीषा *bhīṣā* - Out of reverent obedience (fear) or awe अस्मात् *asmāt* - to *Brahman* (source of fear) वात *vāta* - Wind or air पवते *pavate* - moves or blows.
भीषा *bhīṣā* - Out of reverent obedience (of *Brahman*) सूर्य *Sūrya* - Sun उदेति *udēti* - rises.
भीषा *bhīṣā* - Out of reverent obedience अस्मात् *asmāt* - to *Brahman* अग्निः *Agni* - Fire (burns) च *cha* - and इन्द्रः *Indra* - *Indra* (governs) च *cha* - and,
मृत्युः *mṛtyuh* - Death, पञ्चम *pañchama* - the fifth, धावति *dhāvati* - hastens or rushes इति *iti* - Thus, in this manner, it is said.

Simple translation:

8.1 ***Out of reverence to Brahman, the Wind blows,***
8.2 ***Out of reverence to Brahman, the Sun rises,***
8.3 ***Out of reverence to Brahman, the Fire burns, and Indra governs,***
8.4 ***Out of reverence to Brahman, the Death, the fifth amongst them, hastens.***

These five principles in the Universe are governed by the ऋत (ṛta), the cosmic law or harmony set by *Brahman.*

Philosophical Interpretation:

In *Bhakti*, the divine awe (*bhīṣā*) is inseparable from *kṛpā* (grace). That which inspires reverence also bestows protection.

8.1 Out of reverence to *Brahman*, the Wind blows. Here, Wind is indicative of breath. This can be seen to be related to the *prāṇamaya* sheath.

"*Who could even breathe or live (if not for that Self)?*"

So, when one experiences this Truth, one comes to enjoy that,

8.1 "The Wind blows through us as breath, that stablises our mind, only by His grace".

8.2 Out of reverence to *Brahman*, the Sun rises. Sun is representative of knowledge and illumination. This can be seen as related to the *manōmaya* sheath.

In the Gayatri mantra, we pray "*Oh! Bhargō (Sun), Enlighten our intellect, so that we may realise Thy Supreme Light.* This should be understood as "*Let us meditate upon the Ātman (who shines as the inner light) to illumine the buddhi*". This Truth makes one enjoy the understanding that

8.2 "By His (*Ātman* or *Brahman*) grace alone, the Sun (illumination or knowledge) rises in our *buddhi*". This is responsible for our cognition.

8.3 Out of reverence to *Brahman*, the *Agni* (Fire) and *Indra* (mind) perform their functions. These can be seen to be related to both the *manōmaya* and *vijñānamaya* sheaths.

Here, *Agni* is indicative of the Fire of knowledge, where in, the various *vrittis* such as past impressions and memories are burnt away, rendering the *Chitta* pure. *Indra* represents the mind that governs all the senses and their functionality, which gives one the 'I'-identity responsible for *kartrutwa* (feeling of performing various actions) and *bhoktrutwa* (enjoying the fruits of actions performed), which in Truth are both belonging to the *Brahman.*

When these are understood, the reverence or awe transforms into *bhakti*, and one enjoys the beautiful *bhāvam* (a feeling or emotion beyond the realm of logic), that

8.3 (a) "By His grace, the *Agni*, Fire of wisdom, burns away our impure thoughts of duality arising out of body consciousness and renders the *Chitta* pure".

8.3 (b) "By His grace alone, *Indra*, the reflected consciousness in the mind enjoys the roles of acting and enjoying". Thus the ego is eliminated and one realises that the Brahman alone is the real *Kartru* (Doer) and *Bhoktru* (Enjoyer).

8.4 Out of reverence to *Brahman*, Death, the fifth amongst them, hastens. This can be seen as related to the *ānandamaya* body.

Here, Death is that of individual self, which immediately results in the birth of the One Self.
This is what makes the seeker experience *Ānanda*, the ultimate Bliss, the nature of *Brahman.* It can not be achieved without His grace.

8.4 "By His grace, the dissolution of the individual self, the fifth state, after the four facets of the mind *(manas, buddhi, chitta, Ahaṃkāra)*, are refined, hastens".

This premise sets forth an appropriate background that is required for a detailed discussion on the levels of *Ānanda.*

Summary

As a background to the analysis of the levels of *Ānanda*, the following is stated:

1. *Out of fear of Brahman, the Wind blows*
2. *Out of fear of Brahman, the Sun rises*
3. *Out of fear of Brahman, the Fire burns*
4. *Out of fear of Brahman, Indra governs*
5. *Out of fear of Brahman, the Death hastens*

Having concluded that the *Brahmavid* on becoming *Brahman* has attained an absolute state of fearlessness, why would one reflect on the aspects of fear due to which the laws of nature function?
The reflection on these is indeed the validation of the inner methodology of refining the inner instruments of *(manas, buddhi, chitta, ahaṃkāra)* as one transitions to

the inner four layers from the physical layer, as one turns inward.

Based on the interpretaions of the five sheaths, these can be understood as follows:

1. *By His Grace alone, the Wind blows through us as breath, and stablises the manas.*
2. *By His grace alone, the Sun rises in the buddhi as knowledge and illumines it.*
3. *By His Grace alone, the Fire burns away the impressions and renders the chitta pure.*
4. *By His Grace alone, Indra, ahaṃkāra aspect of the mind, the I-identity or ego, which gives one the feeling of acting and enjoying, is finally eliminated.*
5. *By His Grace alone, the Death of individual self, and the birth of the One Self within, hastens.*

These five stages set forth the required background for understanding the various levels of *Ānanda* that are to follow.

Ānanda Mīmāṁsa

सैषाऽऽनन्दस्य मीमांसा भ॒वति।

saiṣhā (a)nan'das'ya mīmāgṁ'sā bhavati [8.5]

युवा स्यात्साधुयुंवाऽध्या॒यकः। आशिष्ठो दृढिष्ठों बलि॒ष्ठः।
तस्येयं पृथिवी सर्वा वित्तस्यं पूर्णा॒स्यात्॒। स, एको मानुषं, आन॒न्दः।

yuvās' syāt'sādhuyuvā'dh'yāyakaḥa [8.6]
āśhiṣh'ṭhō dṛḍhiṣ'ṭhō baliṣhṭhaḥa [8.7]
tas'yeyaṁ' pṛthivī sar'vā vit'tas'ya pūr'ṇās syā-te [8.8]
sa, ēkō mānuṣha, ānandaḥa [8.9]

ते ये शतं मानुषां, आन॒न्दाः।
स एको मनुष्यगन्धर्वाणांमान॒न्दः।
श्रोत्रियस्य चाकामंहत॒स्य।

tē yē śhataṁ mānuṣhā, ānandā-ḥa [8.10]
sa, ēkō manuṣh'yagan'dhar'vāṇāmānan'daha [8.11]
śhrōt'riyas'ya chākāmahatas'ya [8.12]

ते ये शतं मनुष्यगन्धर्वाणांमान॒न्दाः।
स एको देवगन्धर्वाणांमान॒न्दः।
श्रोत्रियस्य चाकामंहत॒स्य।

tē yē śhatan' manuṣh'yagan'dhar'vāṇāmānandā-ḥa [8.13]
sa, ēkō devagan'dharvāṇāmānan'daḥa [8.14]
śhrōt'riyas'ya chākāmahatas'ya [8.15]

ते ये शतं देवगन्धर्वाणांमान॒न्दाः।
स एकः पितृणां चिरलोकलोकानांमान॒न्दः।
श्रोत्रियस्य चाकामंहत॒स्य।

tē yē śhatan' devagan'dharvāṇāmānan'dā-ḥa [8.16]
sa eka[fp]' pitṛṇāñ' chiralōkalōkānāmānan'daḥa [8.17]
śhrōt'riyas'ya chākāmahatas'ya [8.18]

ते ये शतं पितृणां चिरलोकलोकानांमान॒न्दाः।
स एक आजानजानां देवानांमान॒न्दः।
श्रोत्रियस्य चाकामंहत॒स्य।

tē yē śhatan' pitṛṇāñ chiralōkalōkānāmānan'dā-ḥa [8.19]
sa, ēka ājānajānān' dēvānāmānandaḥa [8.20]
śhrōt'riyas'ya chākāmahatas'ya [8.21]

ते ये शतम् आजानजानां देवानांमान॒न्दाः।
स एकः कर्मदेवानां देवानांमान॒न्दः।
ये कर्मणा देवानंपिय॒न्ति। श्रोत्रियस्य चाकामंहत॒स्य।

tē yē śatam ājānajānān' devānāmānandā-ḥa [8.22]
sa, ēka[hk]' kar'madēvānāṁ devānāmānandaḥa [8.23]
ye kar'maṇā devānapiyan'ti [8.24]
śhrōt'riyas'ya chākāmahatas'ya [8.25]

ते ये शतं कर्मदेवानां देवानांमान॒न्दाः।
स एको देवानांमान॒न्दः। श्रोत्रियस्य चाकामंहत॒स्य।

tē yē śhatan' kar'madēvānāṁ dēvānāmānandā-ḥa [8.26]
sa, ēkō dēvānāmānandaḥa [8.27]
śhrōt'riyas'ya chākāmahatas'ya [8.28]

Mānusha Ānanda

सैषाऽऽनन्दस्य मीमांसा भ॒वति।

saiṣhā anan'das'ya mīmāgṁ'sā bhavati [8.5]

सैषा *saiṣā* - This indeed, आनन्दस्य *ānandasya* - of ānanda (Bliss) मीमांसा *mīmāṃsā* - inquiry, investigation, deliberation, systematic analysis भवति *bhavati* - is / becomes or follows.

8.5 ***"This is the inquiry into Bliss."***
or "Now, the deliberation on the nature of Bliss follows."

युवा स्यात्साधुयुंवाऽध्या॒यकः। आशिष्ठो दृढिष्ठोंबलि॒ष्ठः।
तस्येयं पृथिवी सर्वा वित्तस्यंपूर्णा॒स्यात्॥

yuvās' syāt'sādhuyuvā'dh'yāyakaḥa [8.6]
āśhiṣh'ṭho dṛḍhiṣ'ṭho baliṣhṭhaḥa [8.7]
tas'yēyaṁ' pṛthivī sar'vā vit'tas'ya
pūr'ṇās syā-te [8.8]

युवा *yuvā* - A youth or young person स्यात् *syāt* - may be (let there be) साधु *sādhu* - noble or virtuous young person, अध्यायकः *adhyāyakaḥ* - one who is well-versed in the scriptures (especially *Vēdas*) आशिष्ठः *āśiṣṭhaḥ* - very determined, full of initiative दृढिष्ठो *dṛḍhiṣṭho* - very resolute, mentally strong बलिष्ठः *baliṣṭhaḥ* - physically strongest तस्य *tasya* - For that person, इयम् *iyam* - this पृथिवी सर्वा *pṛthivī sarvā* - the entire Earth, referring to the physical body वित्तस्य पूर्णा *vittasya pūrṇā* - filled with wealth of health स्यात् *syāt* - may be (possessing)

8.6-8.8 ***"Let there be a young man, a noble youth, well-versed in the scriptures, very determined, mentally and physically strongest, and possessing wealth of good health."***

स एको मानुष आनन्दाः।
sa ēkō mānuṣha ānandāḥ [8.9]

स *sa* - This is एको *ēkō* - one unit of मानुष *Mānuṣa* - Human आनन्दाः *Ānandāḥ* - Bliss

8.9 ***This constitutes one unit of mānuṣa ānanda (MA) or Human Bliss.***

That is, one unit of human Bliss is that of a young person, who is blessed with a strong physical body with all the senses working, is well read, mentally strong, is of good character, and is bestowed good health.

One would think that this covers everything one could ask for as a human being. And yet, the deliberations begin to unravel greater levels of Bliss as one uncovers the layers of their personality. The first step in this direction is that these human beings have to worship or meditate upon *Brahman* (*yē'nnaṁ brahmopāsatē* [2.8]). That is, one's life has to turn the direction from outward to inward. As long as one is driven by the external world, despite all achievements, their Bliss is limited and is of a fleeting nature, as they continue to suffer from the cycle of birth and death. Those who realise that the purpose of human life is to go back to the source from where one has come, the inward journey back to the *Brahman* begins.

Manushya Gandharva Ānanda

ते ये शतं मानुषांनुन्दाः

tē yē śhataṁ mānuṣhā ānandāḥ **[8.10]**

ते *tē* - Those ये *yē* - who possess शतं *śataṃ* - a hundred times of मानुषा *mānuṣā* - human आनन्दाः *Ānandaḥ* - Bliss

8.10 *Those who possess a hundred times of Mānu-ṣhā Ānanda or Human Bliss*

स एको मनुष्यगन्धर्वाणांमानुन्दः

sa, ēkō manuṣh'ya gan'dhar'vāṇām ānan'daha **[8.11]**

स *sa* - That person has एको *ēkō* - one unit of मनुष्यगन्धर्वाणामानन्दः *manuṣya gandharvāṇām ānandaḥa.*

8.11 That person has one unit of *Manuṣya Gandharva Ānanda* (1 MGA)
1 MGA = 100 MA = 10^2 MA

Gandharva has root word *gandha* - smell, fragrance and suffix as *-rva* / *-rvaṇa* - sound or movement. So, *Gandharvas* are those connected with fragrance and music. Symbolically, *Gandharvas* are identified with the vital breath or *prāṇa* (Chāndogya Up. 8.6.6).

Manushya Gandharvas are considered as refined human beings who, through *gandharva vidhya*, that is, through control of prāṇa or vital breath, elevate their human consciousness towards divinity.

Typically, *Gandharvas* are those who possess knowledge and skill of various arts, such as music, dance, sculpture, painting, etc. Human beings enjoy these art forms to gain happiness. One certainly enjoys listening to music, watching good drama, and dancing. One also might be a connoisseur of the arts, such as painting and sculpture. These are all foods taken through various senses that nourish us. But, the true Bliss is accrued only when one directs these towards the worship or contemplation of *Brahman.* One must use one's hands to perform worship of the divine, legs to circumambulate the divine, mouth to glorify the Lord's story, eyes to be always pining for the Lord's darshan, ears to listen to the bhajans or music that glorifies the divine, etc. When one is consumed by such divine activities, one attains the Bliss, called *Manushya Gandharva Ānanda* (MGA).

8.11 ***The Bliss obtained through utilisation of one's organs of action and perception in worship of the divine is Manushya-Gandharva Ānanda.***

श्रोत्रियस्य चाकामहतस्य।

śrotriyasya chā kāmahatasya [8.12]

श्रोत्रियस्य *śrotriyasya* - of one learned in the Vēdas; च *cha* - and; अकामहतस्य *akāmahatasya* - desireless, free from passion;

8.12 ***Such a person who is well versed with the Vēdas and is not touched by worldly desires (proceeds further).***

Dēva Gandharva Ānanda

ते ये शतं मनुष्यगन्धर्वाणांमानन्दाः

tē yē śhataṁ'
manuṣya gandharvāṇām ānandāḥ [8.13]

8.13 Those who possess a hundred times more of *Manuṣya-Gandharva Ānanda.*

स एको देवगन्धर्वाणांमानन्दः

sa, ēkō dēvagandharvāṇām ānandaha [8.14]

8.14 *That person has one unit of Dēva-Gandharva Ānanda (1 DGA).*

1 DGA = 10^2 MGA = 10^4 MA

Every human being is blessed with a certain innate talent, be it in music (*gāna-gandharvās*), dance and drama (*nātya-gandharvās*), painting, sculpting, literary, etc. All these involve either organs of action or those of perception. When one perfects these talents through practice and concentration and directs them for glorification of the divine, they attain the Bliss which is equivalent to *dēva gandharvās.*

For example, the chief of *Gandharvās* is called *Chitraratha*, (*chitra* meaning splendid and *ratha* meaning chariot), the splendid chariot or vehicle. This body is considered to be a chariot with the senses as the horses, the mind as the reins, and the intellect as the *sarathi* (charioteer) and the *ātman* as the rider (*Katha Upaniṣad*

1.33.4) [25]. A splendid chariot is indeed one whose horses are strong and controlled, and the vehicle well maintained. Horses tend to constantly move and have a similar nature to the mind. So, here the mind needs to be stabilised by controlling the breath to become *Chitraratha.* It indicates the culmination of *prāṇamaya kośa*, which bestows this level of *Ānanda.*

That's why we observe that all the talents, in *Bharat*, are directed and centered around the glorification of the Lord's stories. Our entire music, both vocal and instrumental, in both traditions of *Carnatic* and *Hindustani*, is saturated with songs composed towards the glorification of the divine. All our dance forms also depict the divine stories. The entire talents of art and architecture revolve around sculpting and painting of the divine and the construction of temples for the divine.

The Bliss obtained through fulfilment of talents, based on organs of action and perception (dēvas), by offering them to the divine, and hence obtaining a steady mind is Dēva-Gandharva Ānanda.

श्रोत्रियस्य चाकामंहतस्य।

śrotriyasya chā kāmahatasya [8.15]

8.15 ***Such a person who is well versed with the Vēdas and is not touched by worldly desires (proceeds further).***

Pitṛṇāṁ Chiralōkalōkānām Ānanda

ते ये शतं देवगन्धर्वाणांमानुन्दाः।

tē yē śhataṁ' dēvagandharvāṇām ānandāḥ [8.16]

8.16 *Those who possess a hundred times of Dēva Gandharva Ānanda.*

स एकः पितृणां चिरलोकलोकानांमानुन्दः।

sa, ēkaḥ pitṛṇāṁ chiralōkalōkānām ānandaha [8.17]

8.17 That person possess one unit of *Pitṛṇāṁ Chiralōkalōkānām Ānanda* (1 PCA).

1 PCA = 10^2 DGA = 10^4 MGA = 10^6 MA

This is the Eternal Bliss of celestial realms, suggesting stability and elevated joy beyond the transient world. It is of the ancestors, considered responsible for continuing the lineage and blessing descendants.

This long-lasting benefit is accrued due to various good deeds performed using organs of action, especially *Vedic* rites like *śrāddha, agnihotra*, etc. This *ānanda* is an outcome of gratitude to our forefathers from whom we have inherited our body, culture (tálents), and family lineage. Our ancestors symbolise the memory, tradition, and cultural continuity, and offering food and water is the way of nourishing and harmonizing with one's roots. This is referred to as *Pitṛ-ṛṇa*, the debt owed to our ancestors, also called *Pitṛ Yajña*. This also includes respect and love that we should show towards our parents and elders.

One must be grateful to one's parents and ancestors, for one has obtained their innate talents through them. Further, we have been provided the opportunity to harness, sustain, and perfect those talents due to their love and blessings. Our Bliss gets multiplied due to the Bliss they experience when we transform ourselves into an elevated state of being.

This is the transition to the spiritual realm, where one has to move from the external world of senses to the inner world of spiritual realization.

The Bliss obtained through fulfilment of one's duties towards their parents and ancestors is Pitṛṇāṁ Chiralokalokanaam Ānanda.

श्रोत्रियस्य चाकामंहतुस्य।

śrotriyasya chā kāmahatasya [8.18]

8.18 *Such a person who is well versed with the Vēdas and is not touched by worldly desires (proceeds further).*

Ajānajānāṁ Dēvānām Ānanda

ते ये शतं पितृणां चिरलोकलोकानांमानन्दाः
tē yē śhataṁ' pitṛṇāṁ
chiralōkalōkānām ānandāḥ [8.19]

8.19 *Those who possess a hundred times the Pitṛṇāṁ Chhiralokalokanaam Ānanda.*

स एकः आजानजानां देवानांमानन्दः।
sa, ēka ājānajānān' dēvānām ānandaha [8.20]

8.20 *That person possess one unit of Ajanajanaam Dēvanaam Ānanda (ADA).*

$$1\text{ ADA} = 10^2\text{ PCA} = 10^4\text{ DGA} = 10^6\text{ MGA} = 10^8\text{ MA}$$

आजानजानां *ājānajānān' - Those who are born even after being born.*

When one undergoes the *Upanayana Saṃskāra* and receives spiritual initiation into the *Gayatri Mantra*, one is called a *dwija* (twice born). The insights arising as a result of engaging the organs of action and perception, in repetition of the Gayatri mantra during the *Sandhya Vandana*, lead to this level of *ānanda*. This is the level of *ānanda* that would be realised as one reaches and journeys through *Manōmaya kośa.*

These are part of ऋषिऋण *Ṛṣi-ṛṇa* - our debt towards *rishis*, which involves the study, preservation, teaching, and practice of our *Vedic*, cultural, and spiritual traditions. By repaying it thus, not only does one become free from bondage but also gains insight in the form of illumination that "one is the *ātman* and not the body".

The Bliss obtained through attainment of insight, that one is not the body but is truly Self, that is, being born into the inner world of ātman after being born as a human being, is Ajanajanaam Dēvanaam Ānanda.

श्रोत्रियस्य चाकामंहतस्य।

śrotriyasya chā kāmahatasya [8.21]

8.21 ***Such a person who is well versed with the Vēdas and is not touched by worldly desires (proceeds further).***

Karmadēvānām Dēvānām Ānanda

ते ये शतम् आजानजानां देवानांमानन्दाः।

tē yē śatam ājānajānān dēvānāmānandāḥ [8.22]

8.22 *A hundred times that of people who have attained insights as a result of being reborn into the spiritual initiation, after being born.*

स एकः कर्मदेवानां देवानांमानन्दः।

sa, ēka karmadēvānāṁ dēvānāmānandaha [8.23]

8.23 *That person possess one unit of Karmadēvānām Dēvanāmanda (1 KDA).*

$$1\ \text{KDA} = 10^2\ \text{ADA} = 10^4\ \text{PCA} = 10^6\ \text{DGA} = 10^8\ \text{MGA} = 10^{10}\ \text{MA}$$

The *ānanda* due to the development of divine qualities of love and compassion, by engaging the organs of action and perception in activities (*karmani*) saturated with divine nature. These include performance of *yajñas* (sacrifices), Service to God through Service to the needy, etc.

ये कर्मणा देवानंपियुन्ति।

ye karmaṇā dēvānapiyanti [8.24]

ये *ye* - Those who; कर्मणा *karmaṇā* - perform actions देवान *dēvān* - with the senses; अपियन्ति *apiyanti* - to approach (in worship)

8.24 *Those who perform actions with their senses to approach the Brahman in worship.*

These are the ones who utilise their senses to perform

karmas, such as adherence to their duties, performance of *yajñas* for the welfare of the world, devotional worship, offering food to animals, birds, and other creatures, and various other such selfless actions. This is akin to *bhuta yajñaḥ*. This cultivates kindness or compassion (*daya*) towards all beings, and by sharing our love with various living beings, we strive for harmony in the world. This process of offering service to others cleanses us spiritually.

The Bliss obtained through attainment of love and compassion, by performing activities of divine nature (selfless actions) towards all the living beings, is Karmadēvanām Dēvanām Ānanda.

श्रोत्रियस्य चाकामंहतस्य।

śrotriyasya chā kāmahatasya [8.25]

8.25 *Such a person who is well versed with the Vēdas and is not touched by worldly desires (proceeds further).*

Dēvānām Ānanda

ते ये शतं कर्मदेवानां देवानांमानन्दाः।
tē yē śhataṁ karmadēvānāṁ
dēvānāmānandāḥ [8.26]

8.26 ***A hundred times that of people who have attained an illumined state of being through selfless service of others.***

स एको देवानांमानन्दः।
sa, ēkō dēvānām ānandaha [**8.27**]

8.27 That person possess one unit of *Dēva Ānanda* (1 DA).

$$1 \text{ DA} = 10^2 \text{ KDA} = 10^4 \text{ ADA} = 10^6 \text{ PCA} = 10^8 \text{ DGA} = 10^{10} \text{ MGA} = 10^{12} \text{ MA}$$

What is the difference between *Mānuṣa* and *Dēva*?

There is a story in which the *dēvās, manushyās* and *asurās* approach *Brahma* and ask Him for *upadēsha* (instruction) on how to live righteously. *Brahma* uttered a single syllable "*Da*", and the *asurās* understood it as *Daya* (compassion), *manushyās* as *Dāna* (charity), and *Dēvās* took it as *Dama* (control over the senses).

Dēva ānanda is the *ānanda* attained on obtaining complete control over one's senses. This leads to the idea of *Pratyahāra* in the yoga tradition. In fact, such people saturate all their senses with love. Love in their speech filled with Truth, Love in their actions reflected as Dharma, Love in their thoughts felt as Peace, Love in their Character expressed as Ahimsa or Non-violence. Such a life with complete control over one's senses helps one overcome the negative tendencies of *Kāma* (Desire), *Krōdha* (Anger), *Lōbha* (Greed), *Mōha* (Attachment), *Mada* (Pride or Arrogance), and *Matsarya* (Jealousy). This transformation bestows upon them *Dēva Ānanda* (DA), which is a hundred times more than that of KDA.

The Bliss obtained through attainment of control over one's senses, is Dēvānām Ānanda.

श्रोत्रियस्य चाकामंहतस्य।

śrotriyasya chā kāmahatasya [8.28]

Such a person who is well versed with the Vēdas and is not touched by worldly desires (proceeds further).

Indra Ānanda

ते ये शतं देवानांमानन्दः।

tē yē śhatam̐ dēvānām ānandaḥ [8.29]

8.29 *A hundred times that of people who have attained complete control of their senses.*

स एक इन्द्रंस्यानन्दः।

sa ēka, indrasyānanda [8.30]

8.30 *That person possess one unit of Indra Ānanda (1 IA), the Bliss obtained on attaining complete control over their mind.*

$$1\ \text{IA} = 10^2\ \text{DA} = 10^4\ \text{KDA} = 10^6\ \text{ADA} = 10^8\ \text{PCA} = 10^{10}\ \text{DGA} = 10^{12}\ \text{MGA} = 10^{14}\ \text{MA}$$

Indra is considered the King of *Dēvas.* Within the microcosm of human beings, *dēvās* are seen as a representation of *indriyās* and hence, the *adipathi* of *indriyās*, the controller of the senses, the mind, can be considered as *Indra.* In *Bhagavad Gita* (BG-6.34) [19], Arjuna laments

चञ्चलं हि मनः कृष्ण प्रमाथि बलवद्दृढम्।
तस्याहं निग्रहं मन्ये वायोरिव सुदुष्करम्॥

chañchalam̐ hi manaḥ kṛṣṇa pramāthi balavad dṛḍham,
tasyāham̐ nigraham̐ manyē vāyōr iva suduṣkaram.

"O Kṛṣṇa, the mind is indeed unsteady, turbulent, strong, and obstinate. I think it is as difficult to control as the wind."

Kṛṣṇa answers the question (BG-6.35) [19] raised by Arjuna as follows:

असंशयं महाबाहो मनो दुर्निग्रहं चलम्।
अभ्यासेन तु कौन्तेय वैराग्येण च गृह्यते॥

asaṁśayaṁ mahābāhō manō durnigrahaṁ chalam,
abhyāsēna tu kauntēya vairāgyēṇa cha gṛhyatē.

"O mighty-armed Arjuna, undoubtedly the mind is difficult to control and restless. But it can be restrained by practice (abhyāsa) and detachment (vairāgya)."

This control over the mind is attained only through *abhyāsa*, regular practice of meditation, a careful study of our thoughts and intentions (Study More). This should lead to a gradual decrease of one's *sankalpas* (Less Talk), that is, the development of *vairāgya*, detachment. When the mind is thus disciplined, it liberates.

The mind constantly dwells either reminiscing or brooding on the future. One can not control the mind, but one can direct it towards a single object of interest or attention, *Brahman* or the Ultimate Reality, by withdrawing the inputs from various senses, so that it attains one-pointed focus, *Ekāgratā*. This is called *dhyāna* or concentration in the yoga philosophy. This is possible only because one has already attained a steadiness of the mind through control of *prāṇa* and illumination of the mind with the insight that 'one is the ātman and not the body'. One has also attained a level of purity of the *Chitta* through various selfless actions suffused with love and has gained control over one's senses.

The Bliss obtained through attainment of control over one's mind, by obtaining a single pointed focus on the Brahman, is Indra Ānanda.

श्रोत्रियस्य चाकामंहतस्य।

śrotriyasya chā kāmahatasya [8.31]

8.31 ***Such a person who is well versed with the Vēdas and is not touched by worldly desires (proceeds further).***

Brihaspati Ānanda

ते ये शतमिन्द्रंस्यानन्दाः।

tē yē śatam indrasyānandaḥ [8.32]

8.32 *A hundred times more ānanda than that of people who have attained a complete control over their mind.*

स एको बृहस्पतेंरानन्दः।

sa, ēkō bṛhaspatērānandaha [8.33]

8.33 *That person, possess one unit of Brihaspati Ānanda (1 BA), whose intellect is illumined with wisdom, and filled with love, that sees Oneness of the Self amongst all beings.*

$$\begin{aligned}1 \text{ BA} &= 10^2\text{IA} = 10^4 \text{ DA} = 10^6 \text{ KDA}\\ &= 10^8 \text{ ADA} = 10^{10} \text{ PCA} = 10^{12} \text{ DGA}\\ &= 10^{14} \text{ MGA} = 10^{16} \text{ MA}\end{aligned}$$

Bṛhaspati is the *guru* of *Indra* and the *dēvās*, and so one can correlate *Bṛhaspati* as the Intellect. For the mind is always guided by the intellect. *Bṛhaspati* means Lord of expansion, one who expands in Wisdom or Love. So, the true intelligence is the contemplation (*dhārana*) of the Truth that one is the *ātman* and hence to live in *atmic* consciousness (*ātmā tattwam*) by discarding body consciousness. This is reflected as Oneness with nature.

This is referred to as *Dēva Yajña*, one's duty towards Nature.

The Bliss obtained through attainment of an intellect illumined with wisdom and filled with love, is Bṛhaspati Ānanda.

श्रोत्रियस्य चाकामंहतस्य।

śrōtriyasya chā kāmahatasya [8.34]

8.34 *Such a person who is well versed with the Vēdas and is not touched by worldly desires (proceeds further).*

Prajāpati Ānanda

ते ये शतं बृहस्पतेंरानन्दाः।

tē yē śhataṁ' bṛhaspatērānandāḥ [8.35]

8.35 ***A hundred times more ānanda than that of people who have attained wisdom.***

स एकः प्रजापतेंरानन्दः।

sa, ēka prajāpatērānandaha [8.36]

8.36 That person who has one unit of Prajāpati Ānanda (1 PA), is the one who lives with Prajñā, Constant Integrated Awareness (CIA), and thus loves all.

$$\begin{aligned} 1\text{ PA} &= 10^2\text{ BA} = 10^4\text{IA} = 10^6\text{ DA} \\ &= 10^8\text{ KDA} = 10^{10}\text{ ADA} = 10^{12}\text{ PCA} \\ &= 10^{14}\text{ DGA} = 10^{16}\text{ MGA} = 10^{18}\text{ MA} \end{aligned}$$

Here, the being sees the One Self (*Eikyata*), which is the underlying Truth of all Creation. This is true union with God, the purpose of *Yōga* (*yuj* meaning to unite), where one attains *Samādhi*, an intellect (*dhi*) illumined with equal-mindedness (*sama*). In this state, the seeker enjoys everything with an equal-minded attitude, as Lord's *prasādam*, with no attachment whatsoever.

This is referred to as *Brahma Yajña*.

In *Bhagavad Gita* (BG-4.24) [19],

ब्रह्मार्पणं ब्रह्म हविर्ब्रह्माग्नौ ब्रह्मणा हुतम्।
ब्रह्मैव तेन गन्तव्यं ब्रह्मकर्मसमाधिना॥

brahmārpaṇaṁ brahma havir
brahmāgnau brahmaṇā hutam |
brahmaiva tena gantavyaṁ
brahma-karma-samādhinā ||

"The offering is *Brahman*, the oblation is *Brahman*, it is offered by *Brahman* in the Fire of *Brahman*. That person who is absorbed in actions for *Brahman* alone, surely attains *Brahman*."

The Bliss obtained through attainment of Constant Integrated Awareness, is Prajāpati Ānanda.

श्रोत्रियस्य चाकामंहतस्य।

śrotriyasya chā kāmahatasya [8.37]

8.37 ***Such a person who is well versed with the Vēdas and is not touched by worldly desires (proceeds further).***

Brahma Ānanda

ते ये शतं प्रजापतेंरानन्दाः।

tē yē śhatam̐ prajāpatērānandāḥ [8.38]

8.38 *A hundred times more ānanda than that of people who have attained Prajāpati ānanda.*

स एको ब्रह्मंण आनन्दः।

sa, ēkō brahmaṇa ānandaha [8.39]

8.39 *That person who has attained one unit of Brahma Ānanda (1 BA), obtained on dissolving one's Ego, by complete surrender or reaching the state of Supreme Love.*

$$\begin{aligned} 1\ \textit{BrahmaĀnanda} &= 10^2 \text{ PA} = 10^4 \text{ BA} = 10^6\text{IA} \\ &= 10^8 \text{ DA} = 10^{10} \text{ KDA} = 10^{12} \text{ ADA} \\ &= 10^{14} \text{ PCA} = 10^{16} \text{ DGA} = 10^{18} \text{ MGA} \\ &= 10^{20} \text{ MA} \end{aligned}$$

The Bliss obtained on becoming Brahmavid, is Brahma Ānanda.

Finally, the *ahaṃkāra* (Ego) is dissolved and the seeker ceases to exist, reaching a state of *amanaskam* (no mind). The Ego having dissolved, there is no second, leaving the seeker in a state of absolute fearlessness. The seeker loses his individual identity and attains the nature of *Brahman*, which is supreme Bliss (*Param*). That is, *Brahmavid* attains *Supreme Bliss.* This is the ultimate Bliss, which is taken to be 100 times that of *Brihaspati Ānanda*, and is called *Brahma Ānanda*, but in reality, one can not quantify it. It is Infinite, which is not quantifiable. This indeed is our true nature, *Satchidānanda*: *Brahman* is Existence as pure Consciousness with Infinite Bliss.

श्रोत्रियस्य चाकामंहतस्य।
śrotriyasya chā kāmahatasya [8.40]

8.40 *Such a person who is well versed with the Vēdas and is not touched by worldly desires (proceeds further).*

The Microcosm and The Macrocosm

स यश्चांयं पुरुषे। ***sa yaśchāyaṁ puruṣē*** [8.41]

स यश्चायं *sa* - The Seeker *yaśchāyaṃ*- thus journeys (to the Ultimate Reality), पुरुषे। *puruṣē* - within the *puruṣa*.

8.41 *Thus, one journeys into the Puruṣa, to the Ultimate Reality.*

यश्चासांवादित्ये। ***yaśchāsāvādityē*** [8.42]

य *ya* - That *Brahman*, the Ultimate Reality (that exists within the individual being) च chā - and आसाव् *asāv* - that which exists (within) आदित्ये *ādityē* - in the Sun (as well)

8.42 That same Ultimate Reality, which is within Oneself, is that which exists in the Sun, also.

One can understand the reference to Sun, for one has experienced the Ultimate Reality as *ādityavarnam*, the supreme effulgence as that of the Sun.

स एकः। sa, ēkah [8.43]

स (sa) - The Ultimate Reality एकः (ēkaḥ) - is "One"

8.43 *The Ultimate Reality is "One"*.

स यंएवंवित्। sa ya ēvaṁvit [8.44]

स य sa ya - Thus One does; एवंवित् (ēvaṁvit): knows this (Truth of One Self that pervades everything, everywhere, and at all times.)

8.44 *Thus one comprehends the unity of the Ultimate Reality within themselves and that in the Cosmos*.

That is,
अणोरणीयान् महतोमहीयान्
aṇōr aṇīyān mahatō mahīyān.
aṇōr aṇīyān: Infinitely subtle; beyond sensory perception, atomic, pervading even the tiniest aspects of reality.
mahatō mahīyān: Infinitely great; encompassing all Creation, transcending the Universe, beyond all concepts of vastness.

The Inward Journey

अस्माल्लोंकात्प्रेत्य। ***asmāllōkātprētya*** [8.45]

अस्माल्लोकात् *asmāllōkāt* - अस्मिन *asmin* - "in this," and लोक *loka* - "world" or "realm." प्रेत्य *prētya* - comes from प्रति *prati* - "towards" + अय *aya* - "going".

8.45 *This indicates the transition from one state or realm to another*

एतमन्नमयमात्मानमुपसङ्क्रामति।
ētamannamayamātmāna mupasaṅkrāmati [8.46]

एत *ēta* - This आत्मानम् *ātmanam* - Self (that is undergoing a transition) उपसङ्क्रामति *upasaṅkrāmati* - moves toward or transitions.

सङ्क्राम् *saṅkrām* - to cross; उप *upa* - closer to. So, it implies a transition or movement closer to a new state.

8.46 *This Self transitions from annamaya and moves closer to prāṇamaya.*

एतं प्राणमयमात्मानमुपंसङ्क्रामति।
ētaṁ prāṇamayamātmāna mupasaṅkrāmati [8.47]

8.47 *This Self transitions from prāṇamaya and moves closer to Manōmaya.*

एतं मनोमयमात्मानमुपंसङ्क्रामति।
ētaṁ manōmayamātmāna mupasaṅkrāmati [8.48]

8.48 ***This Self transitions from manōmaya and moves closer to vijñānamaya.***

एतं विज्ञानमयमात्मानमुपंसङ्क्रा॒मति।

ētaṁ vijñānamayamātmāna
mupasaṅkrāmati [8.49]

8.49 ***This Self transitions from vijñānamaya and moves closer to ānadamaya.***

एतमानन्दमयमात्मानमुपंसङ्क्रा॒मति।
तदप्येष श्लोंको भ॒वति॥

ētamānandamayamātmāna
mupasaṅkrāmati [8.50]

8.50 ***This Self transitions from ānandamaya and moves closer to the state of Brahman.***

This Self transitions from *annamaya*, the physical form, to *prāṇamaya*, that of vital energy, then it transitions from *prāṇa* to *manōmaya*, that of the mind form, following which, it transitions from mind form to *vijñānamaya*, the form of wisdom, further this wisdom form transitions to the *ānandamaya*, state of *ānanda*, and finally it transcends the layer of *ānanda* as well to establish itself in the *Brahman.*

तदप्येष श्लोंको भ॒वति॥

tadap'yēṣhash' śhloko bhavati **[8.51]**

The essence of knowledge and Truth through compact, poetic, and structured language.

Conclusion

यतो॒ वाचो॒ निव॑र्तन्ते। अप्रा॑प्य॒ मन॑सा स॒ह।
आनन्दं॑ ब्रह्म॑णो वि॒द्वान्। न बिभेति कुत॑श्चने॒ति।
एतं॑ग् ह वाव॑ न त॒पति।

yato vācho nivar'tan'tē [9.1]
ap'raāpya manasā saha [9.2]
ānan'daṁ' brah'maṇo vid'vānē [9.3]
na bibhēti kutaśhchanēti [9.4]
ētagṁ' ha vāva na tapati [9.5]

किमहं साधु॑ नाक॒रवम्। किमहं पापमक॑रवमि॒ति।
स य, एवं विद्वानेते, आत्मा॑नंग् स्पृ॒णुते।
उ॒भे ह्ये॑वैष॒, एते, आत्मा॑नंग् स्पृ॒णुते।

kimahaṁ' sādhu nākaravam [9.6]
kimahaṁ' pāpamakaravamiti [9.7]
sa ya ēvaṁ' vid'vānete', āt'mānag'ges' spṛṇutē [9.8]
ubhēh' hyēvaiṣha, ētē ātmānag'gēs' spṛṇutē [9.9]

य, ए॒वं वे॑द। ya, ēvaṃ vēda [9.10]

इत्यु॑प॒निष॑त्॥ it'yupaniṣhatē [9.11]

Final State of *Brahmavid*

यतो वाचो निवर्तन्ते। अप्राप्य मनसा सह।
yatōvāchō nivar'tan'tē [9.1],
ap'raāpya manasā saha [9.2].

यतो *yatō* - From which (or From where) वाचो *vāchō* (Speech or Words) निवर्तन्ते *nivartantē* - The root निवर्त *nivarta-* 'to return' or 'to cease'.
अप्राप्य *aprāpya* - Not attainable, unattainable मनसा *man-asā* - With the mind, by the mind सह *saha* - Together, with

9.1, 9.2 "From which (Brahman) speech returns, along with the mind, not having attained (it)."

This highlights the importance of direct realization, attained through meditation or complete surrender, to the Ultimate Reality, which is beyond the reach of both speech and mind. The *Brahmavid* attains both a state of *nishabdham*, utmost silence, and a state of *amanaskam*, a state of no mind.

आनन्दं ब्रह्मणो विद्वान्। न बिभेति कुतश्चनेति।
ānan'dam̐' brah'maṇō vid'vān [9.3],
na bibhēti kutaśhchanēti [9.4]

आनन्दं *ānandam* - is Bliss ब्रह्मणो *brahmaṇō* - Of Brahman, the Ultimate Reality विद्वान् *vidvān* - Knower.

9.3 The Knower of Brahman is Bliss.

न *na* - Not बिभेति *bibhēti* - (one who) fears कुतः *kutaḥ* -

from anything whatsoever (from anywhere) च *cha* - and नेति *nēti* - not or does not go.

9.4 ***It negates the idea of fear or the act of fearing, implying that not only does the subject not fear, but there is also no movement or reason for fear to exist.***

He does not fear from anywhere (or anyone), nor does he fear at all.

एतंग् ह वाव न तपति। *ētagṁ' ha vāvana tapati* [9.5]

वाव *vāva* - Wow! एतं *ētagṁ* - This person ह *ha* - verily न *na* - does not तपति *tapati* - burn (perform austerities)

9.5 ***Wow! This person, who has realised the Self, verily, does not need to perform any more austerities.***

The realised soul after achieving absolute equanimity becomes immune to destruction/anxiety due to the dualities.

किमहं साधु नाकरवम्।
kimahaṁ' sādhunākaravam [9.6]

किम *kim* - Why अहम् *aham* - did I न *na* - not अकरवम् *akaravam* - not performed साधु *sādhu* - virtuous deeds.

किमहं पापमकरवमिति।
kimahaṁ' pāpamakaravamiti [9.7]
किमहं *kimahaṃ* - Why have I करवमिति *karavamiti* - performed such पापम *pāpa* - sin or wrong actions.

9.6, 9.7 *Why did I not do something virtuous? Why have I performed such a sinful action?*

स य एवं विद्वानेते आत्मानंग् स्पृणुते।

sa ya ēvaṁ' vid'vānētē',
āt'mānag'ges' spṛṇutē [9.8]

स य एवं *sa ya ēvaṃ* - The seekers, who thus (reflect) एते *ētē* - are these विद्वान *vidvān* - Knowers of आत्मानं *ātmānaṃ* - the Self स्पृणुते *spṛṇute* - in touch implies in direct contact, or through direct experience.

9.8 The seekers, who thus reflect, are these Knowers of the Self, through direct experience.

उभे ह्येवैष एते आत्मानंग् स्पृणुते।

ubhēh' hyēvaiṣha, ētē ātmānag'gēs' spṛṇutē [9.9]

उभे *ubhē* - Both (virtuous and sinful actions) हि *hi* - indeed एव *ēva* - are transcended एते *ētē* - by those आत्मानग् स्पृणुते *ātmānages spṛṇutē* - who have established direct contact with the One Self.

9.9 *Those who have established direct contact with the One Self, are the only ones indeed who have transcended, both virtuous and sinful actions.*

य एवं वेंद। ya ēvaṃ vēda [9.10]

य *ya* - Who (a person possessing) एवं *evaṃ* - in this way (the manner or method in which something is perceived or realized) वेद *Vēda* - In this context, it means "knows" or "knows well".

9.10 *It implies that "He who knows thus" or "He who knows in this way" has attained a profound understanding of the Ultimate Reality (Brahman).*

इत्युंपनिषंत्॥ *ityupaniṣat* [9.11]

इति *iti* - Thus concludes (the teaching of the) उपनिषत् *upaniṣat* - उप *upa* - Near or Close by, नि *ni* - Sit (down at the feet of Guru) and षत् *ṣat* - Stay (be there).
This is the way to attain the knowledge of *Brahman.*

9.11 *Thus concludes the teaching of the Upaniṣad.*

Thus concludes the teaching of the Ultimate Reality attained by sitting near the feet of the *Guru* and being (there).

मानस भजरे गुरुचरणम्।
दुस्तर भवसागर तरणम् ॥
mānasa bhajare gurucharaṇam
duṣtara bhāvasāgara-taraṇam.

Oh mind! Worship (take refuge in) the feet of the *Guru*; They are the means to cross the difficult ocean of worldly existence (*saṃsāra*).

ॐ शान्तिः शान्तिः शान्तिः
oṁ śāntiḥ śāntiḥ śāntiḥ

Index

Bibliography

[1] Swami Devrupananda. *Mantra Puṣpam.* Ramakrishna Math, Mumbai, 9th edition, 2013.

[2] Ravi Prakash Arya and Alois Heinrich. *The Vaiśeṣika Darśana: Vedic Physics and Metaphysics of Existing Universe.* Indian Foundation for Vedic Science, Rohtak, Haryana, India, 2024.

[3] Swami Gambhirananda. *Chandogya Upaniṣad.* Advaita Ashrama, Kolkata, 2003. Translated by Swami Gambhirananda.

[4] Swami Dayananda Saraswati. *Taittirîya Upaniṣad*, volume 2. Arsha Vidya Research and Publication Trust, 2016.

[5] A. Mahadeva Sastri. *The Taittirîya Upaniṣad: With the commentaries of Sankarâchârya, Suresvarâchârya and Sâyana (Vidyâranya).* Gyan Publishing House, 2024.

[6] Swami Sarvapriyananda. Youtube video link. `https://youtu.be/Ftn4zCnheBk?si=Ick3HFAw3q6nTOsH&t=450`.

[7] Bhagavan Sri Sathya Sai Baba. The glory of upanishads, divine discourse. https://saisarathi.com/divine-discourses/the-glory-of-upanishads/, 1991.

[8] https://en.wikipedia.org/wiki/Third_ventricle.

[9] Swami Virupakshananda. *Sāṃkhya Kārikā of Isvara Krsna*. Sri Ramakrishna Math, Chennai, 1995. Translated by Swami Virupakshananda.

[10] Keshav Dev Verma. *Vedic Physics: Towards Unification of Quantum Mechanics and General Relativity*. Motilal Banarasidass Publishers, Delhi, 2005.

[11] John Goldthwait. *Purifying the Heart*. Sri Sathya Sai Sadhana Trust, Publication Division, Puttaparthi.

[12] *https://वेद.com/rigvedà/10*.

[13] *https://वेद.com/yajurveda/31*.

[14] R. L. Bijlani and S. Manjunatha. *Understanding Medical Physiology, A Textbook for Medical Students*. Jaypee Brothers Medical Publishers (P) Ltd., New Delhi, 4th edition, 2014.

[15] Cairo Osvaldo. External measures of cognition. *Frontiers in Human Neuroscience*, 5, 2011.

[16] Matrushree Ananthalakshmi et al. *Panchakosha Pathway: Essential Indic Guide to*

Self-Discovery. Anaadi Foundation, Iyvar Malai, North Thathanaickenpatti, Palani Taluk, Tamil Nadu, 2024.

[17] Diwakar Acharya. On the meaning and function of Ādeśá in the early upaniṣads. *Journal of Indian Philosophy*, 45:539–567, 2017.

[18] Govind Dhabolkar (Hemadpant). *Shri Sai Satcharita.* Shri Saibaba Sansthan Trust, 18th edition, January 2018.

[19] Paramahamsa Yogananda. *The Bhagavad Gita: God Talks with Arjuna.* Yogda Satsanga Society of India, first edition, 2009. Vol. 1 & 2.

[20] O. S. K. S. Sastri. A parallel between bhagavad gita shlokas and newton's laws of motion. 1(4):262–269, July-August 2014. Available at: `http://ijmas.com/pastissuedetails.aspx?ID=6`.

[21] Sri Sri Ravi Shankar. *Patanjali Yoga Sutras.* Sri Sri Publications Trust, 2012.

[22] Maunish Vyas. Saivēda.net website. `https://saiveda.net/mv/naaraayaNa_suuktam_en.pdf`.

[23] Bhagavan Sri Sathya Sai Baba. *Treat patients with Love*, volume 28. 1995.

[24] Bhagavan Sri Sathya Sai Baba. *Everyone is a son of God*, volume 15. 1982.

[25] Swami Gambhirananda. *Katha Upaniṣad.* Advaita Ashrama, Kolkata, 2003. Translated by Swami Gambhirananda.